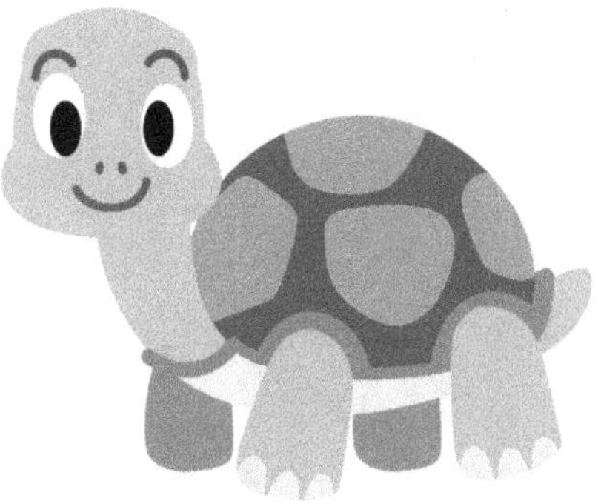

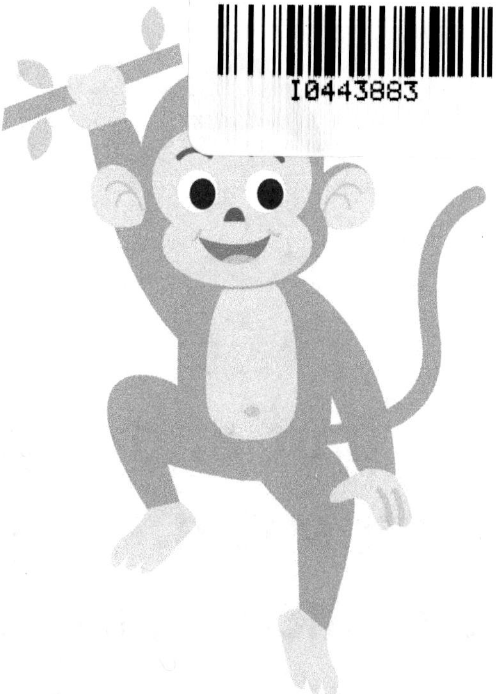

This Book Belongs to:

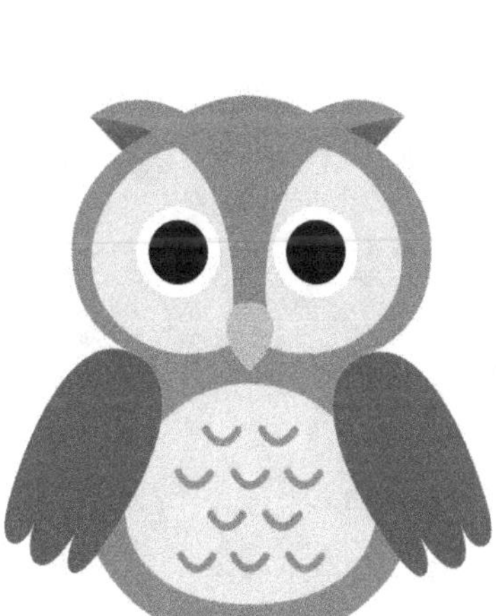

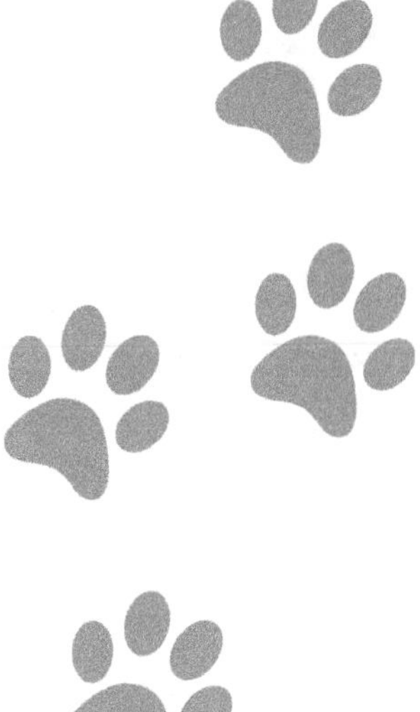

Test Color Page

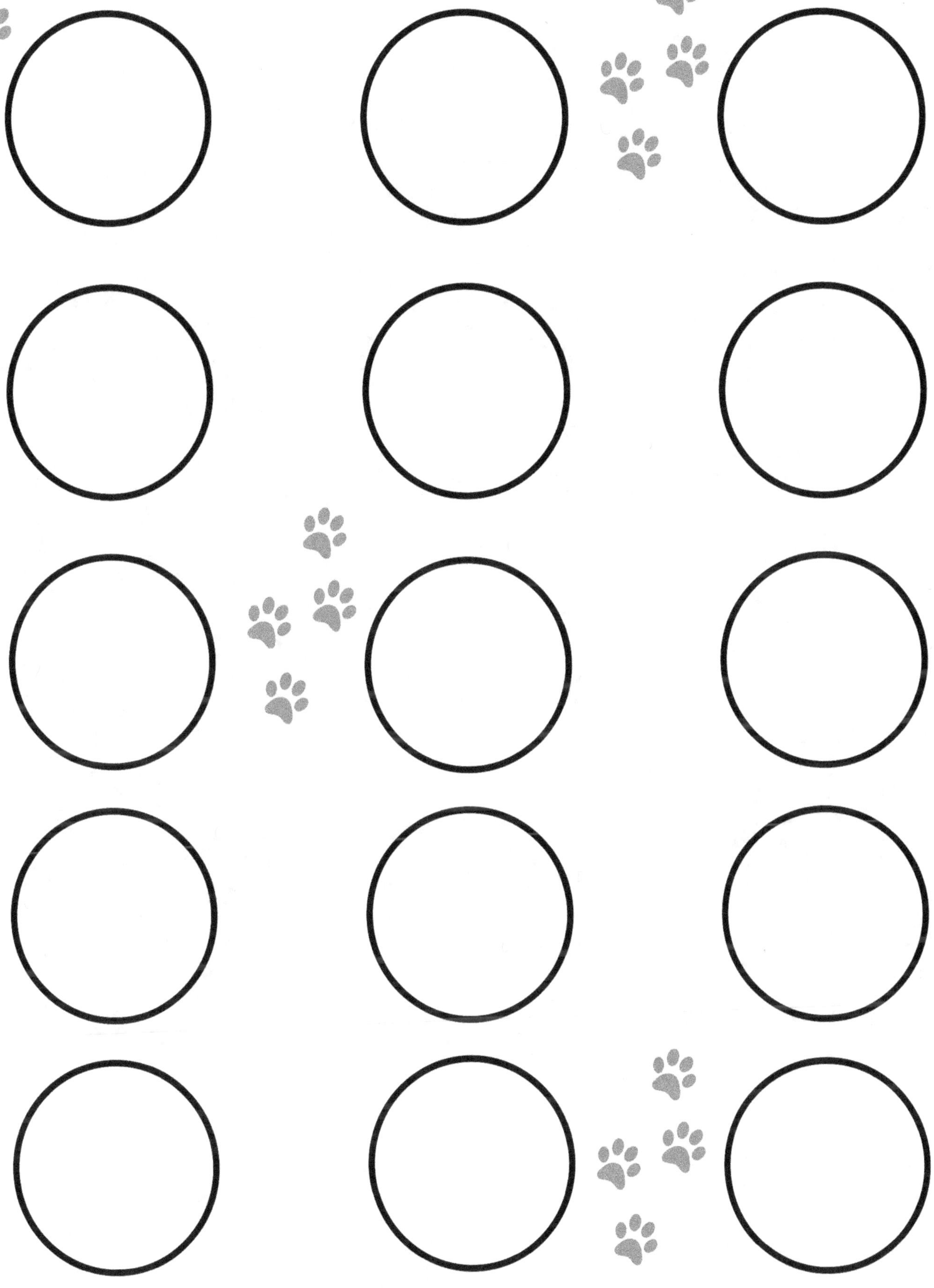

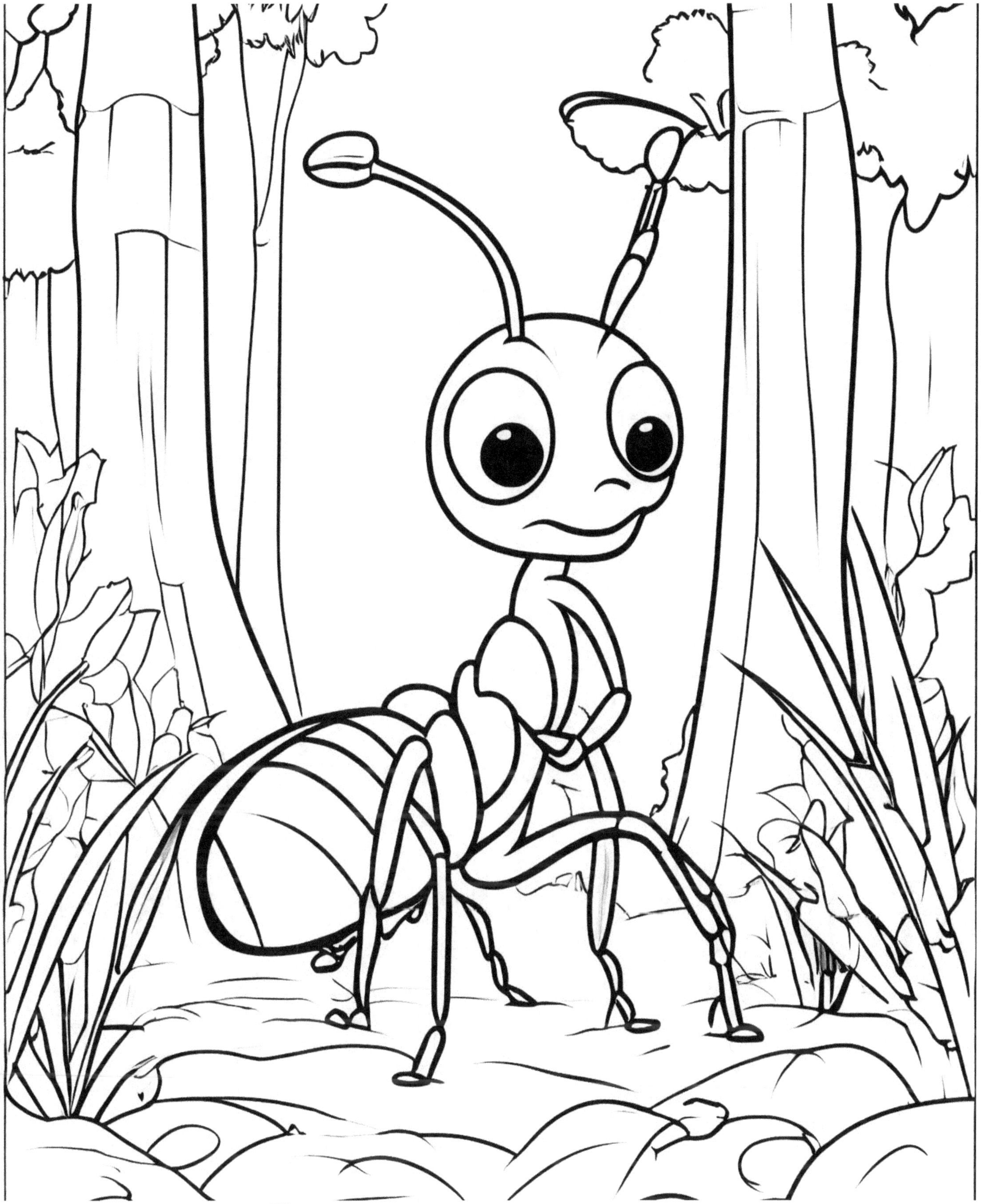

ANT

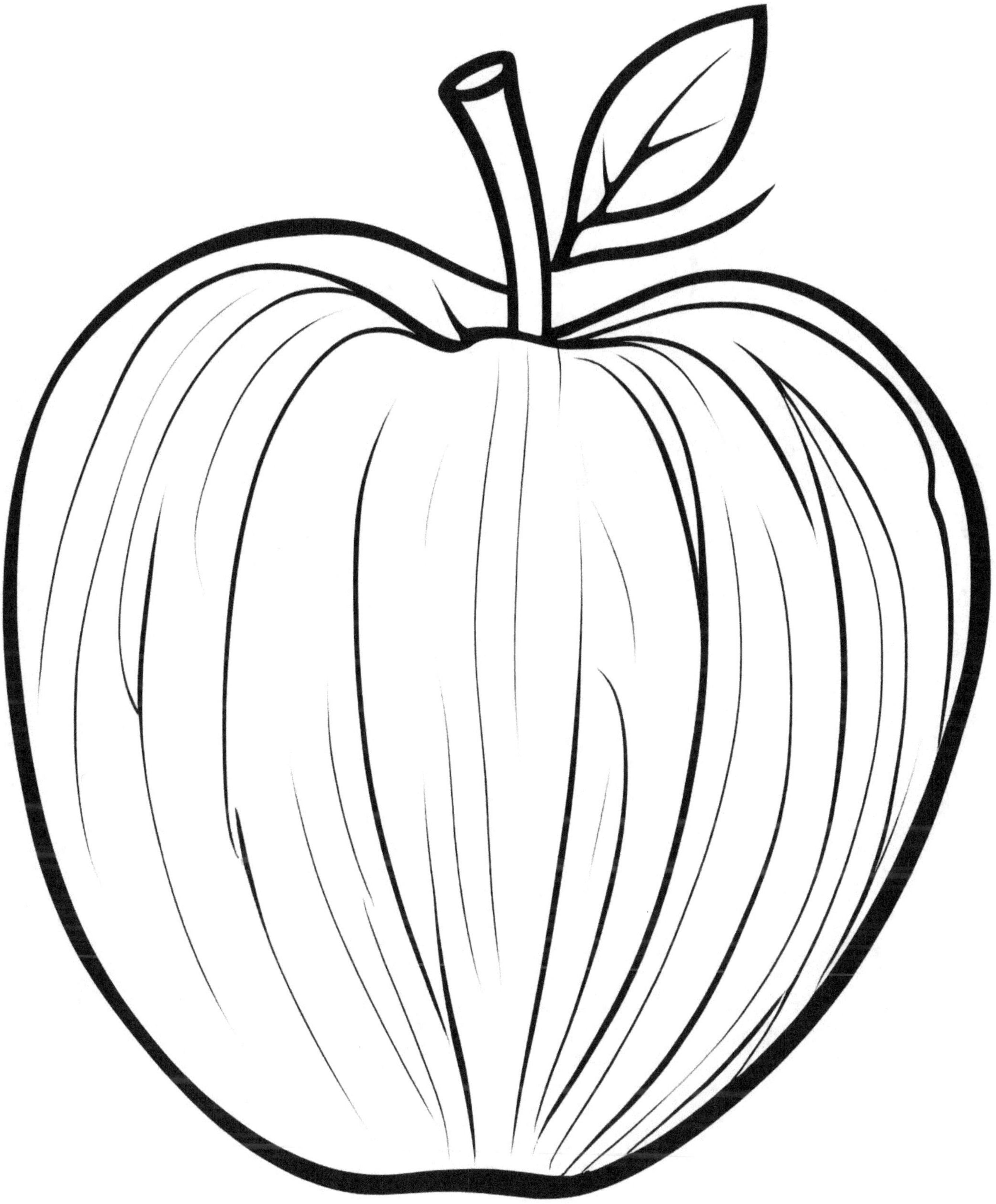

APPLE

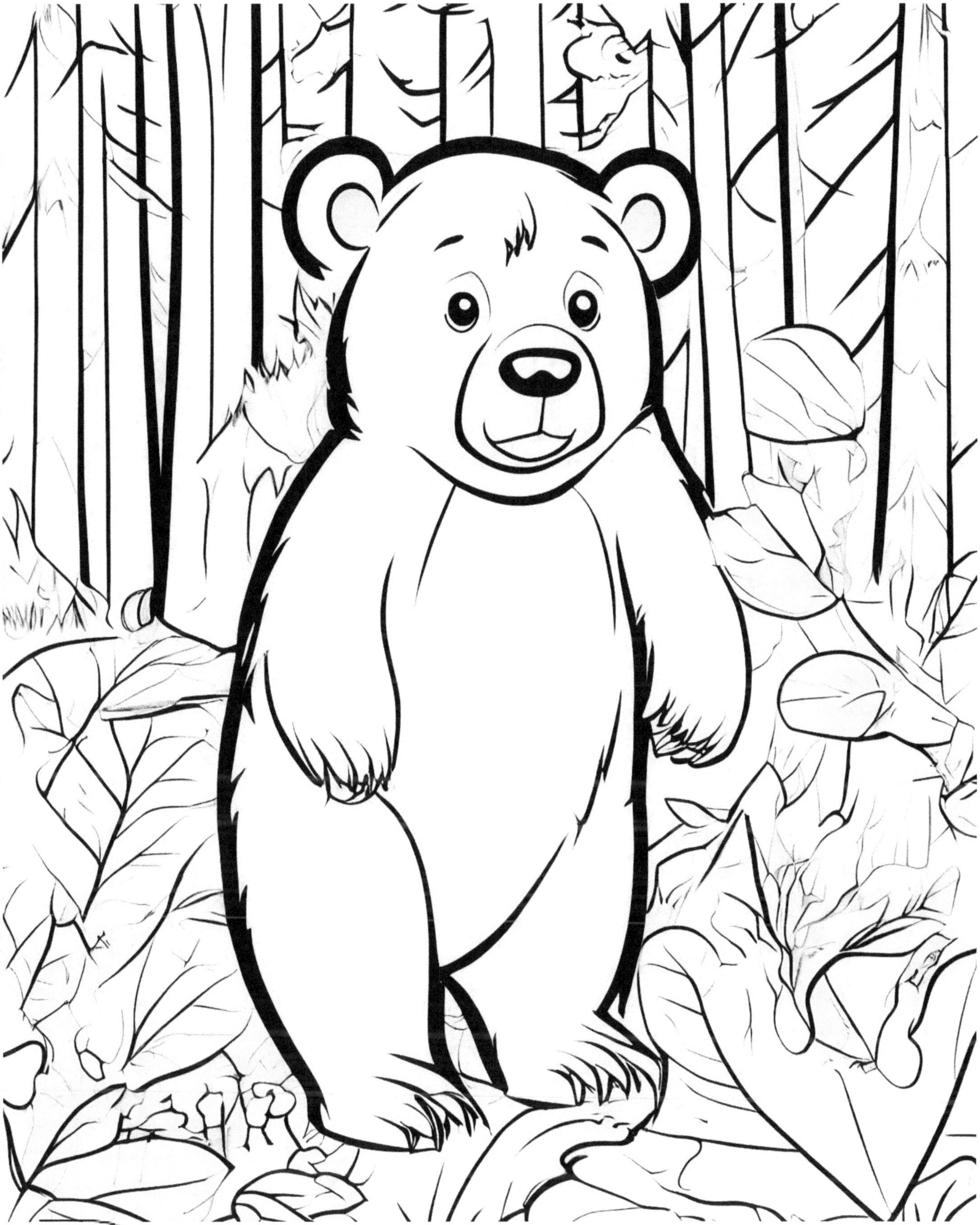

BEAR

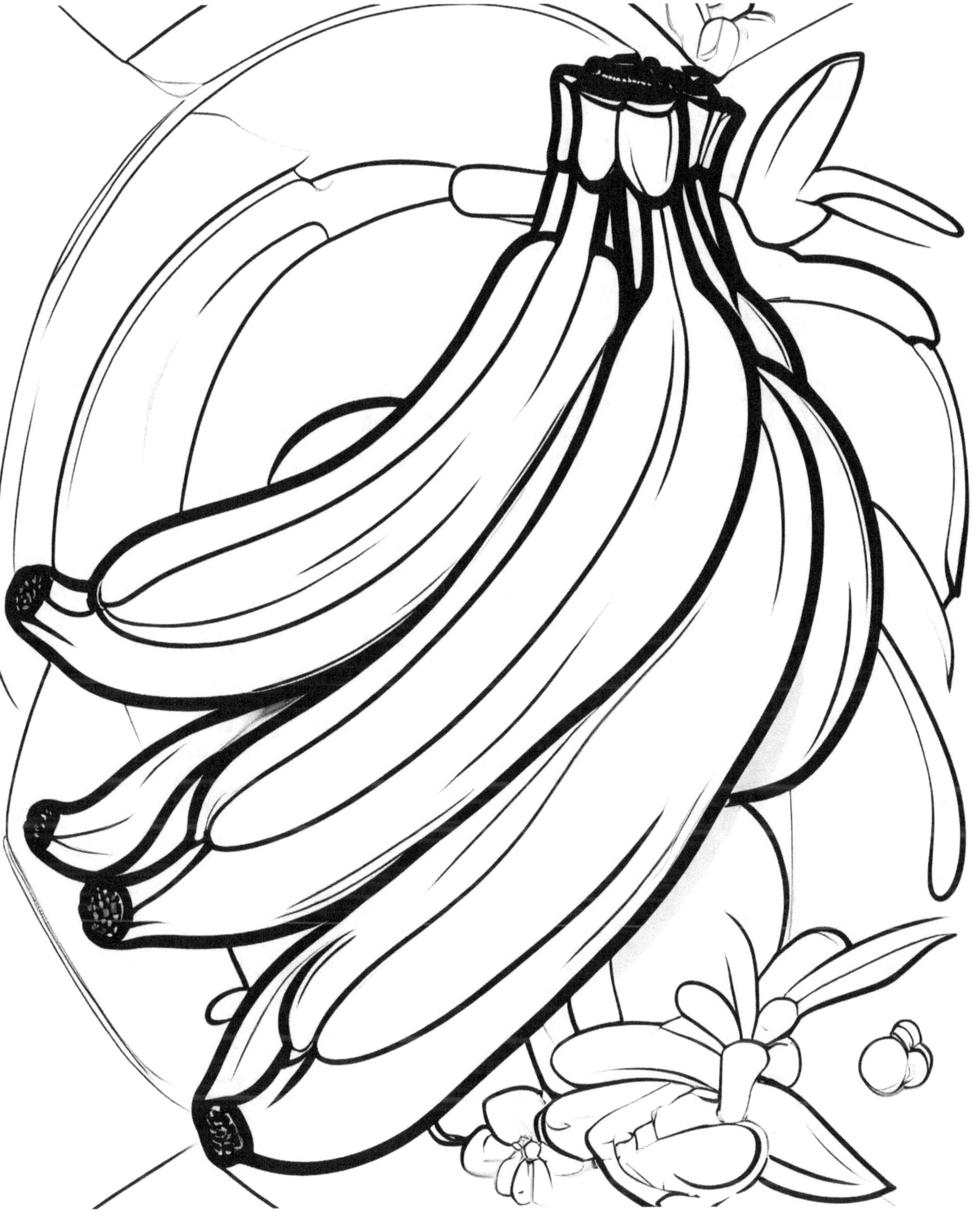

BANANA

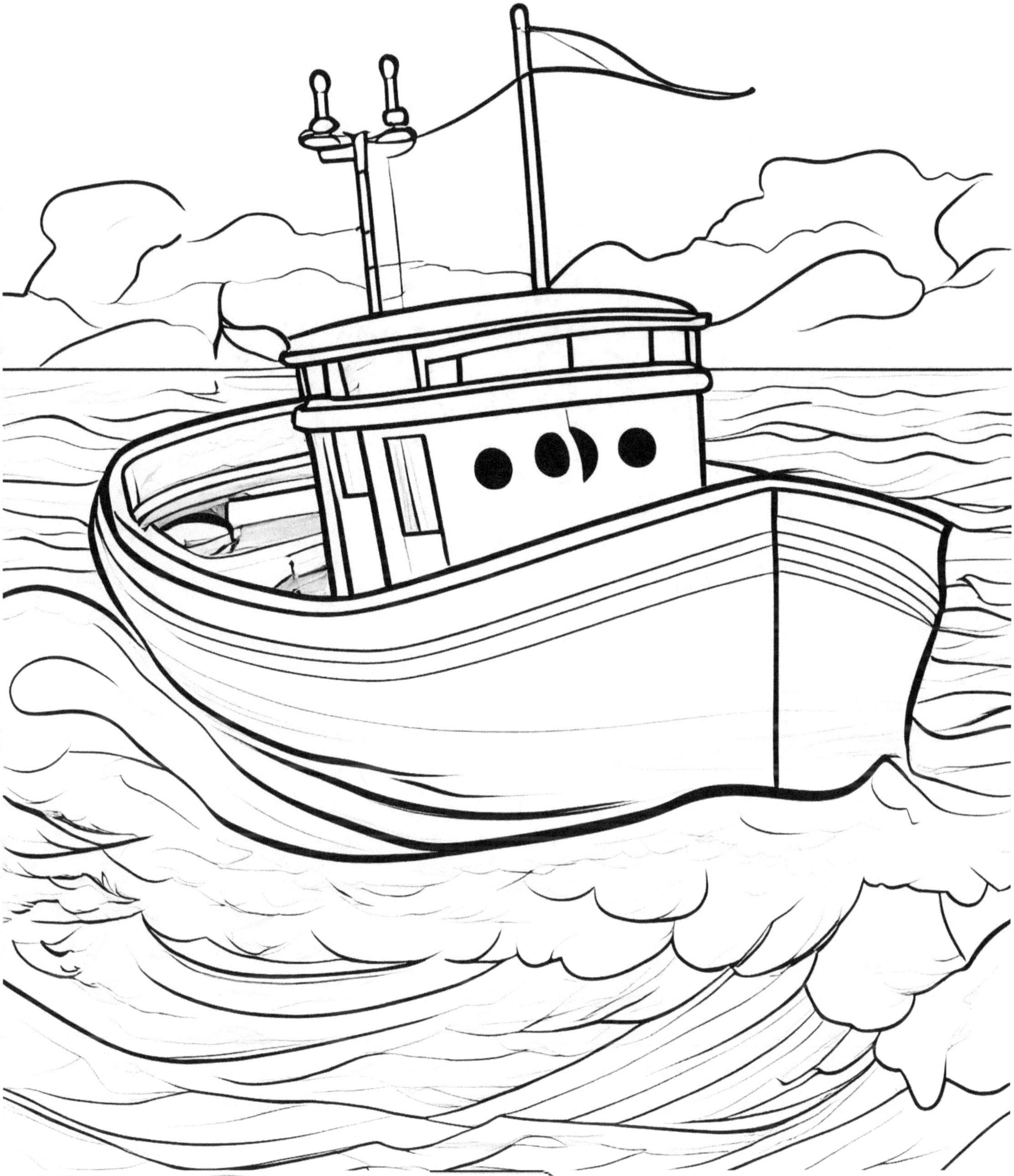

BOAT

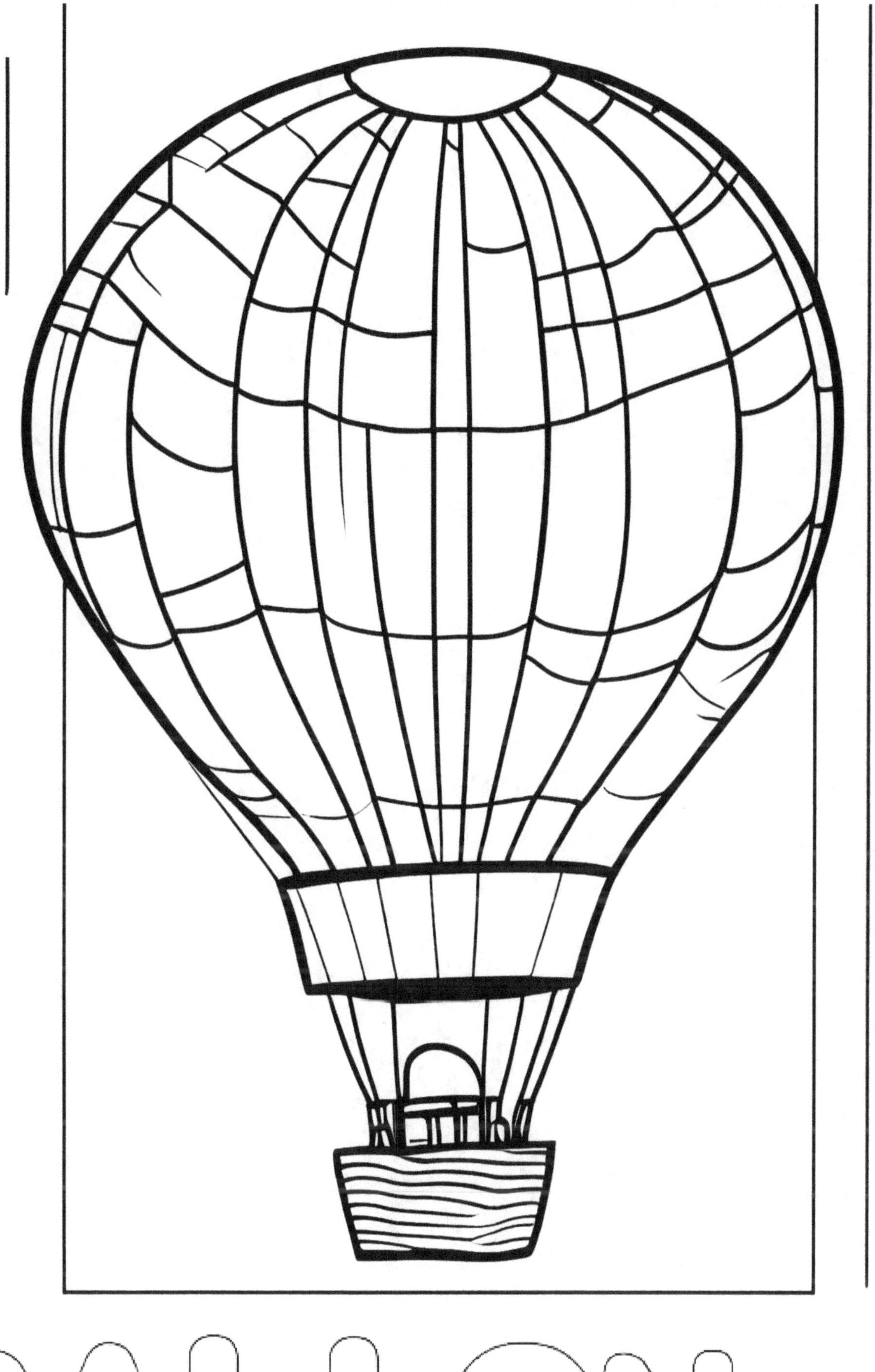

BALLON

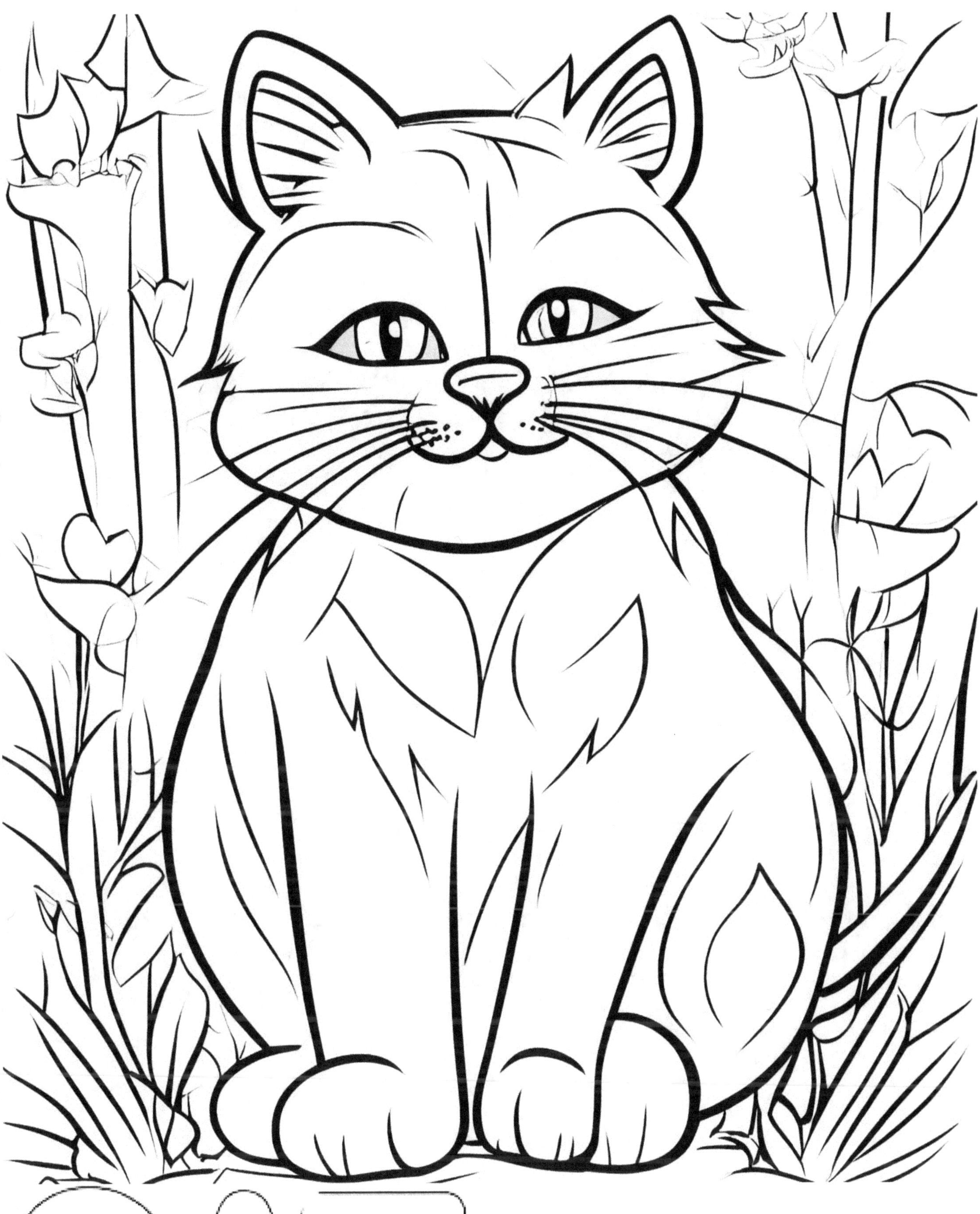

CAT

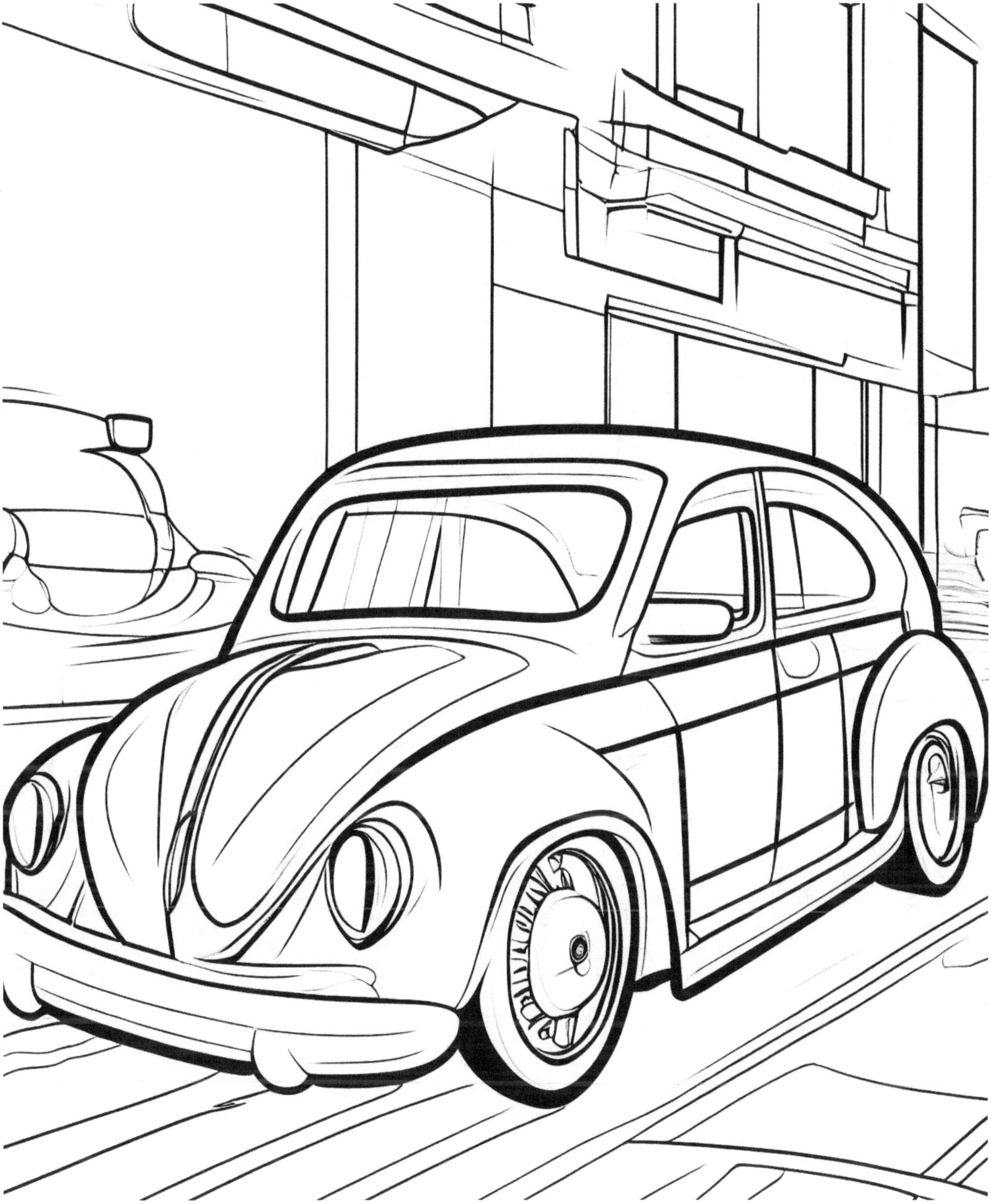

CAR

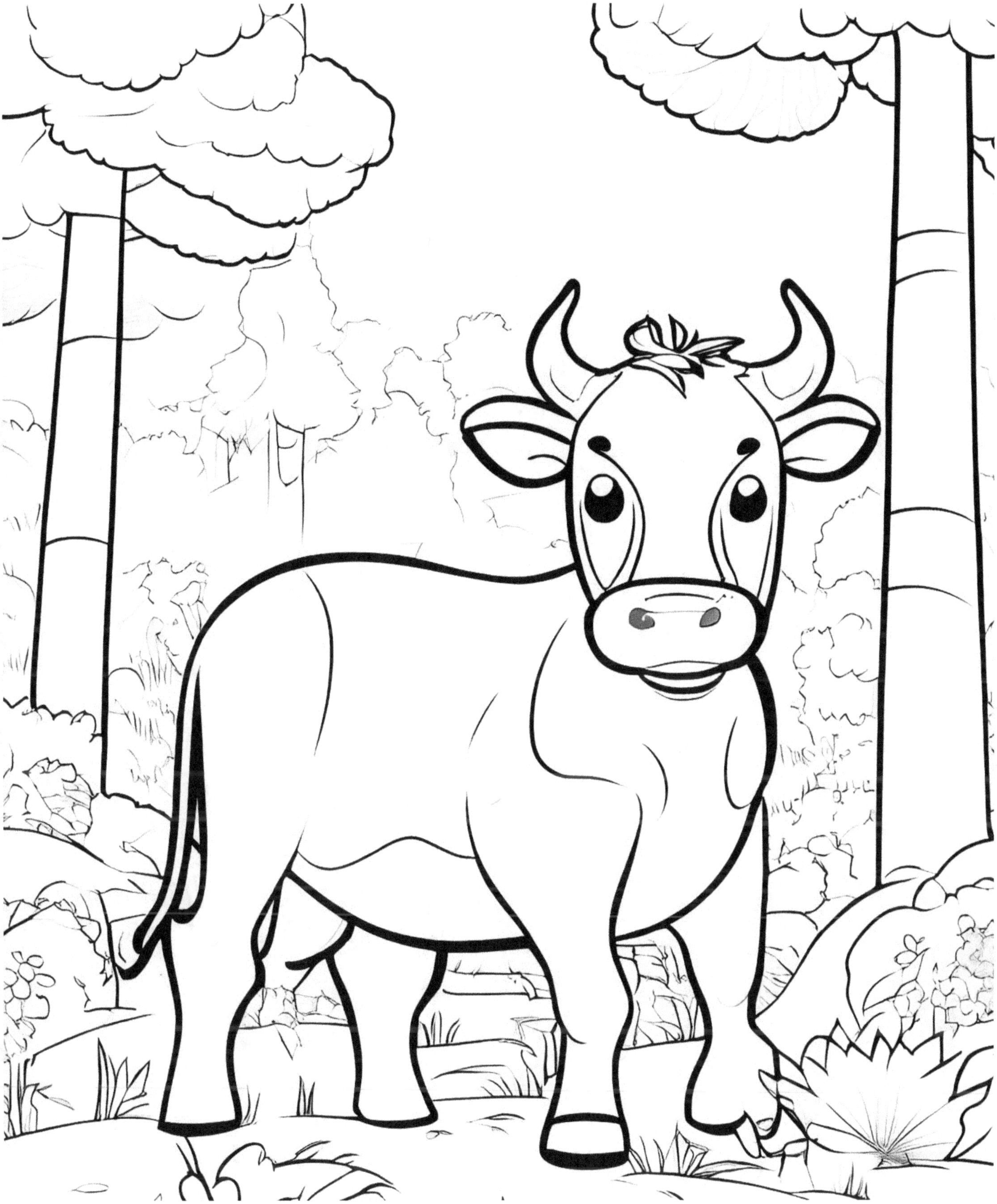

COW

CANDLE

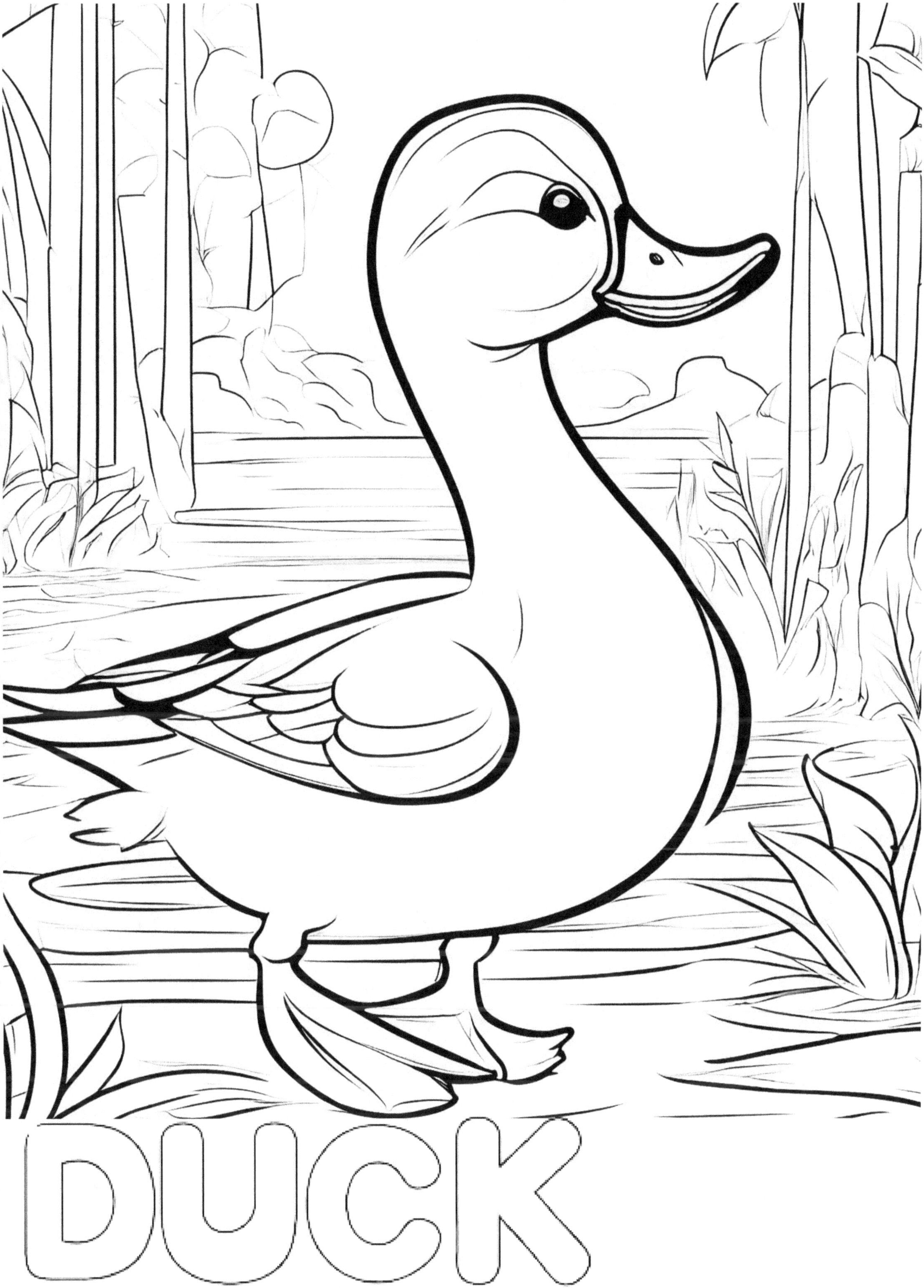

DUCK

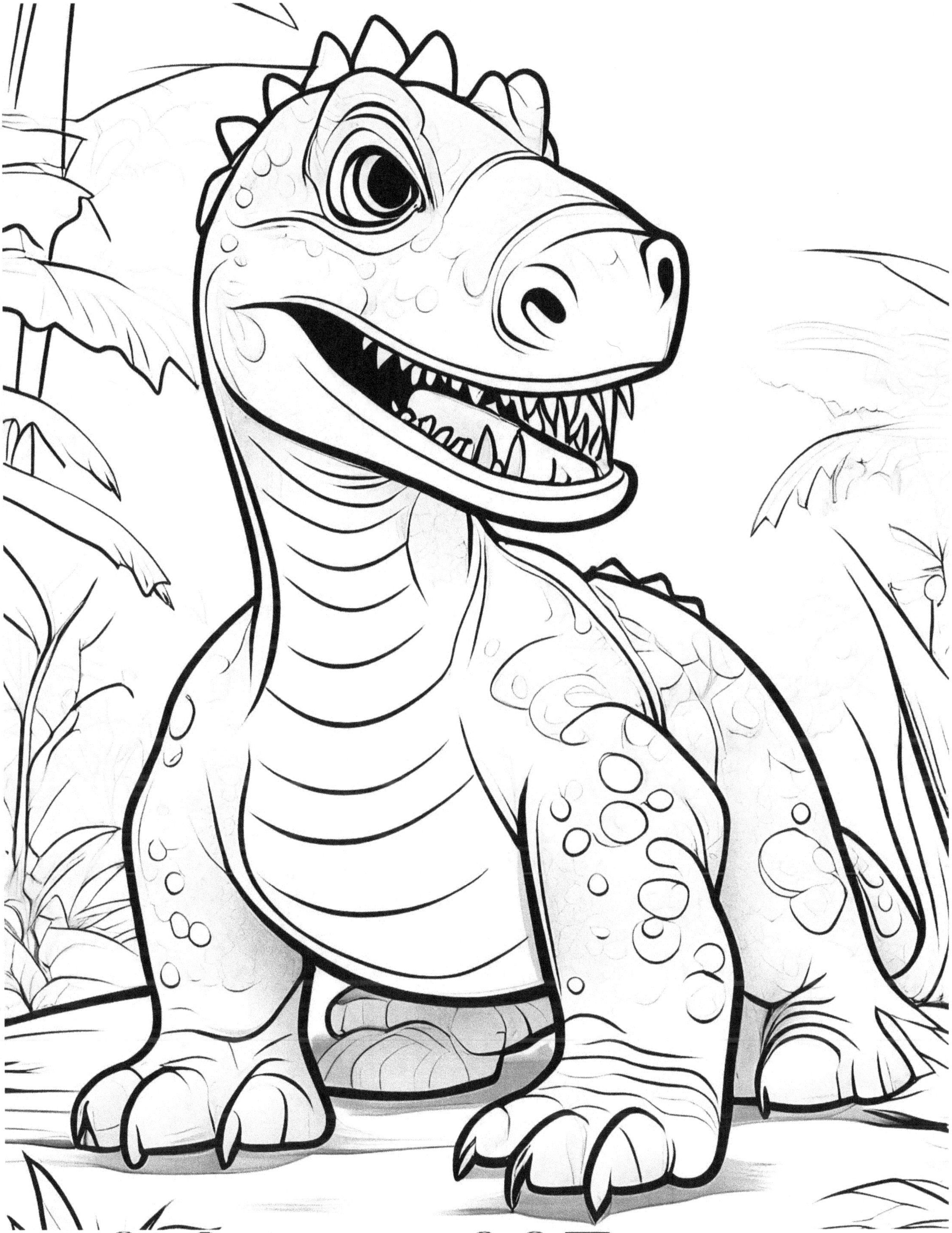

DINOSAUR

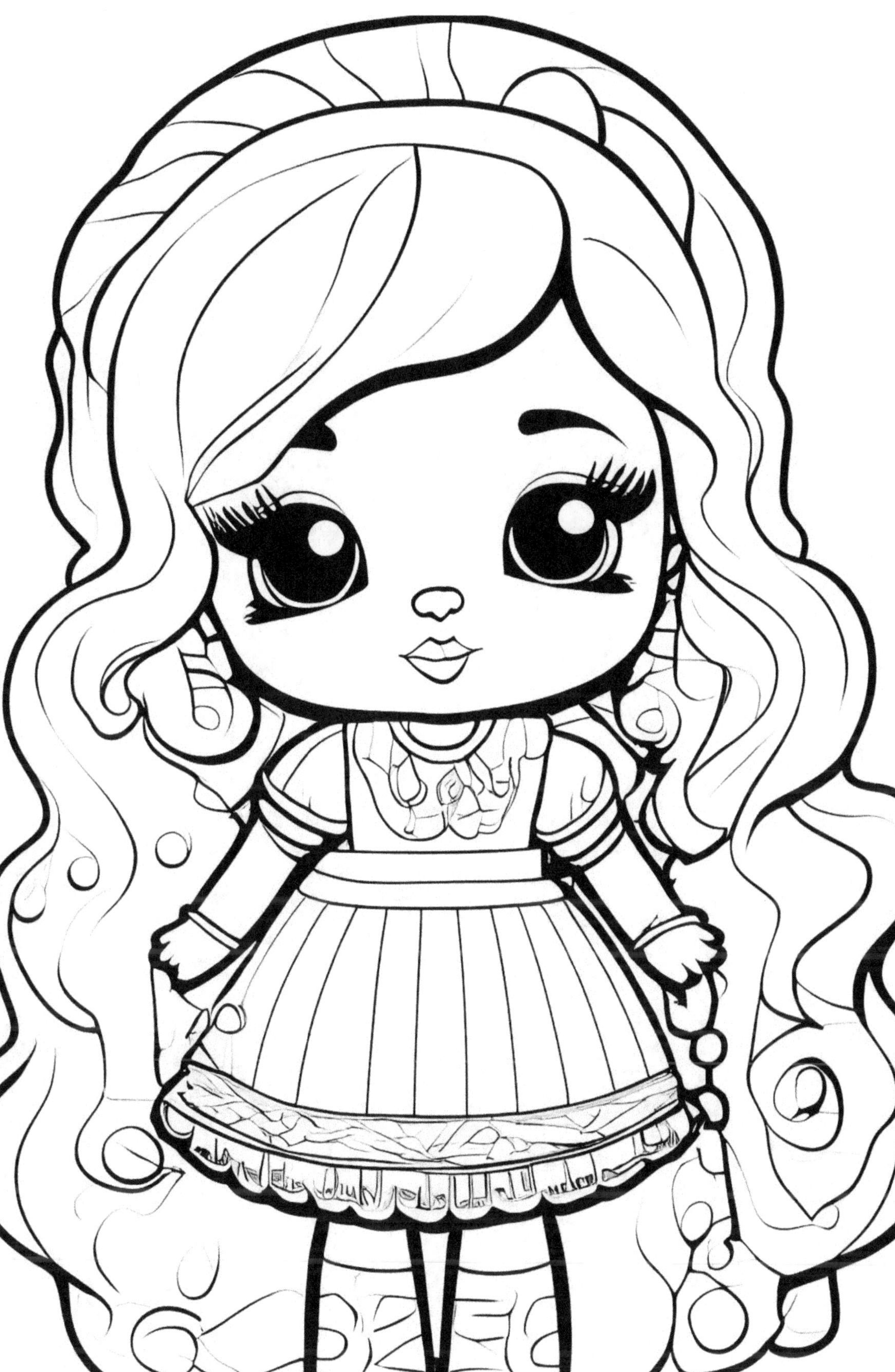

DOLL

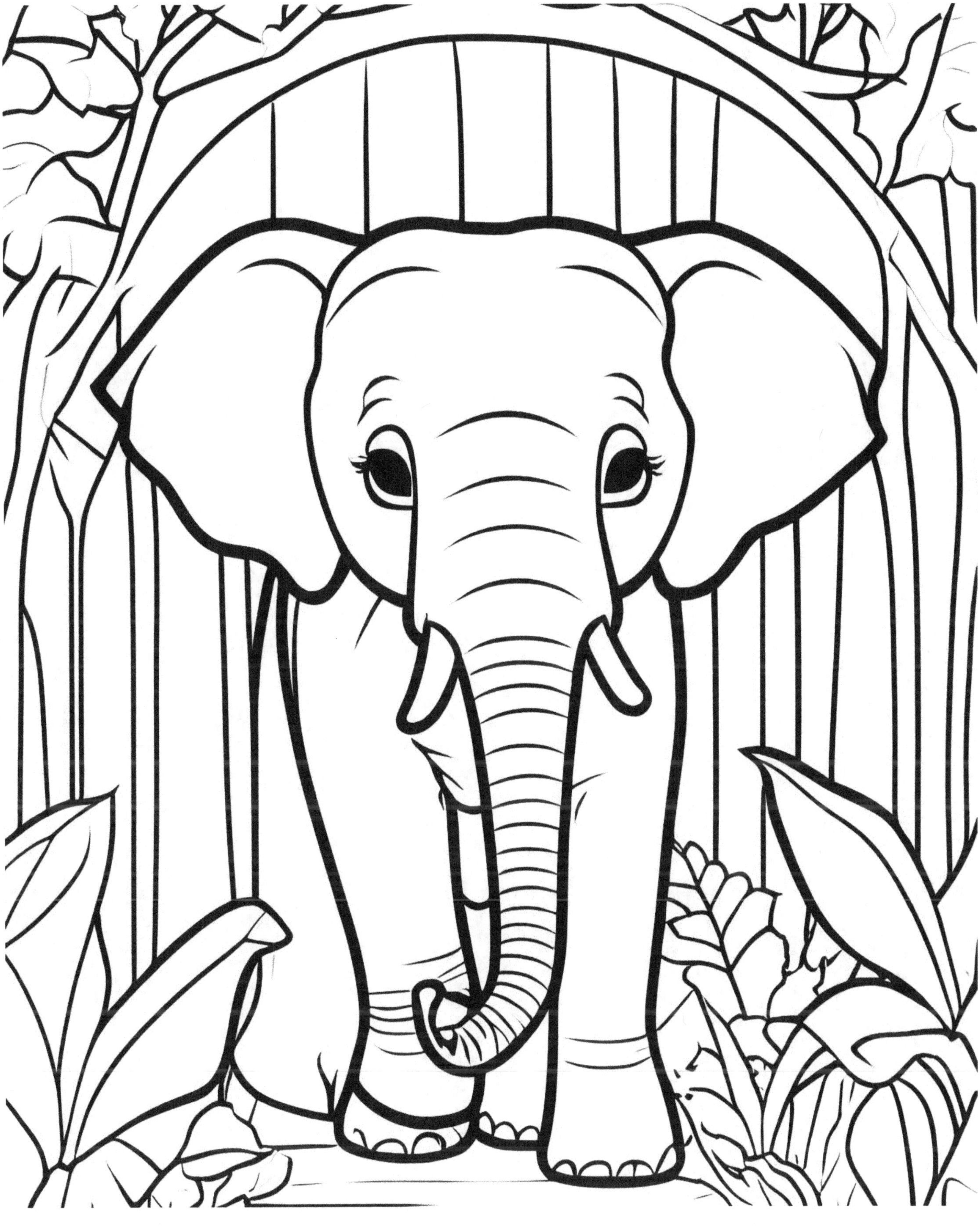

ELEPHANT

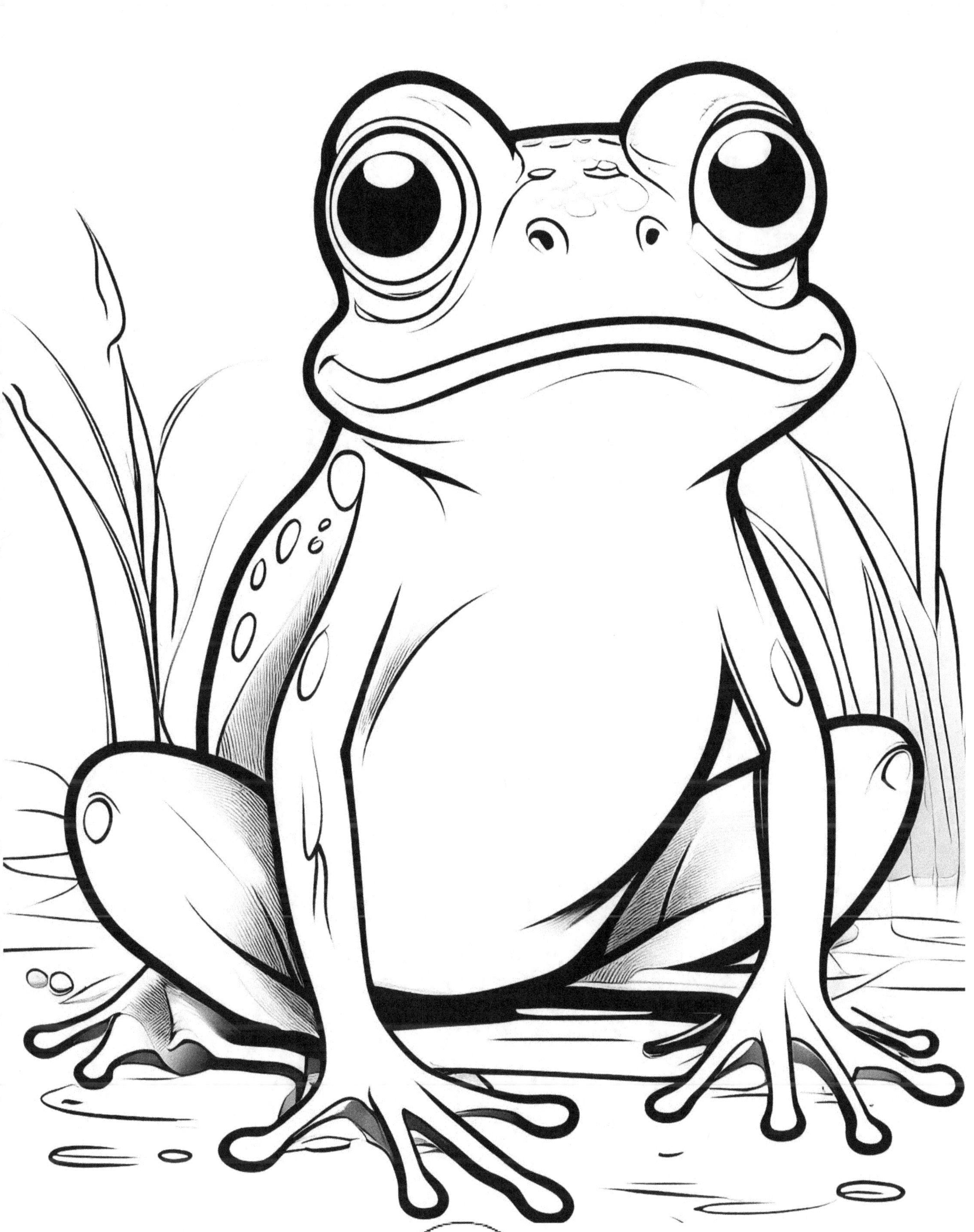

FROG

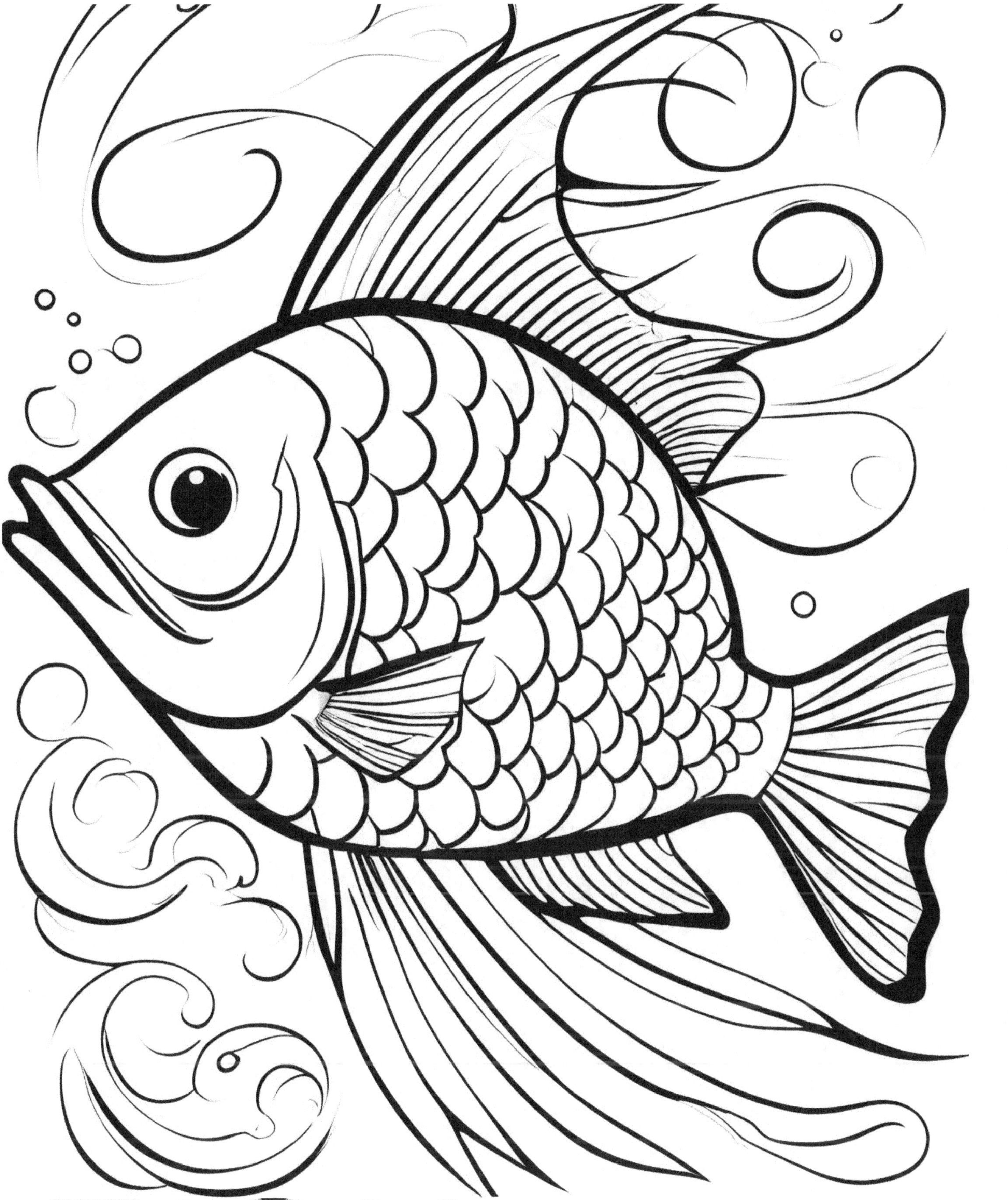

FISH

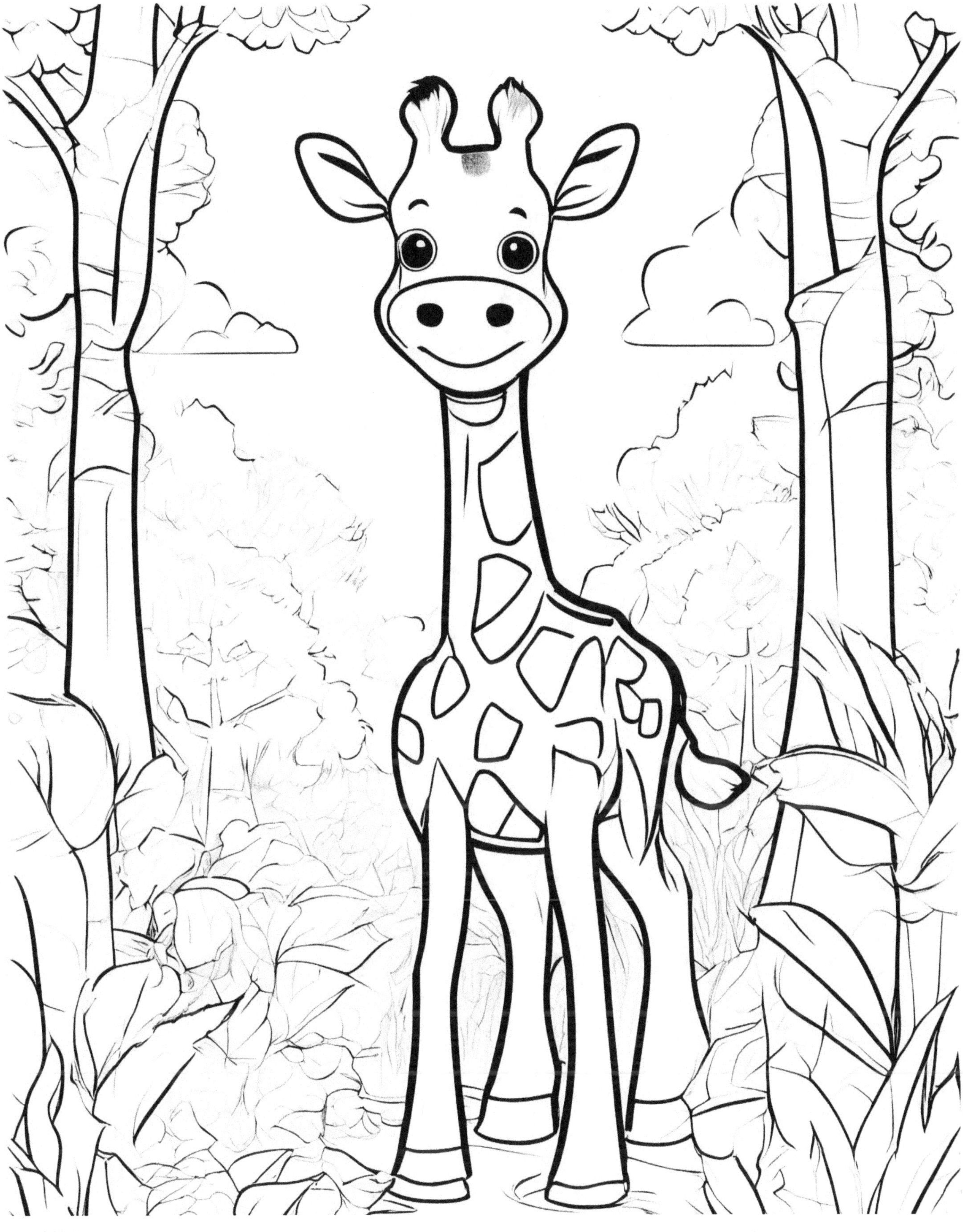

GIRAFFE

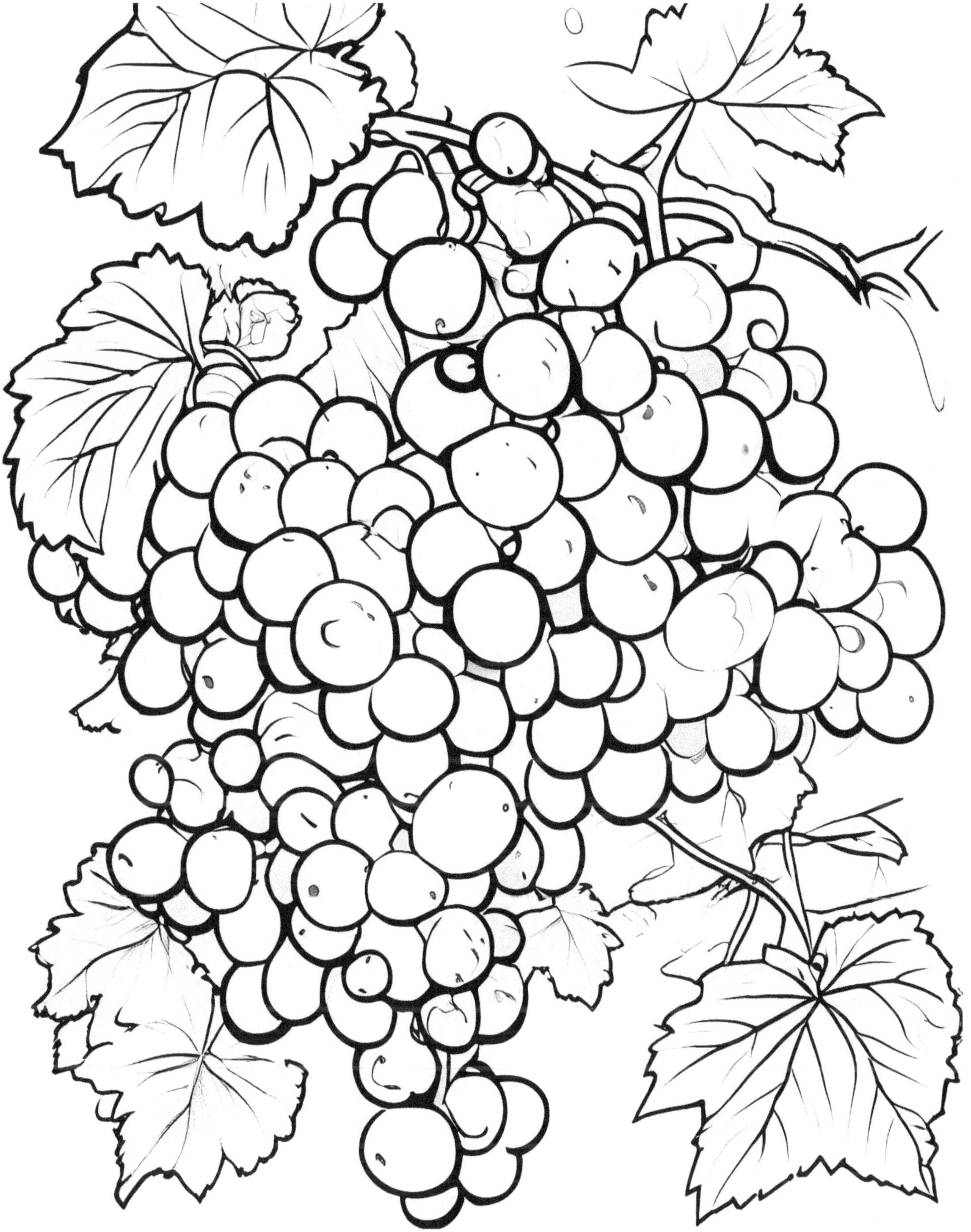

GRAPE

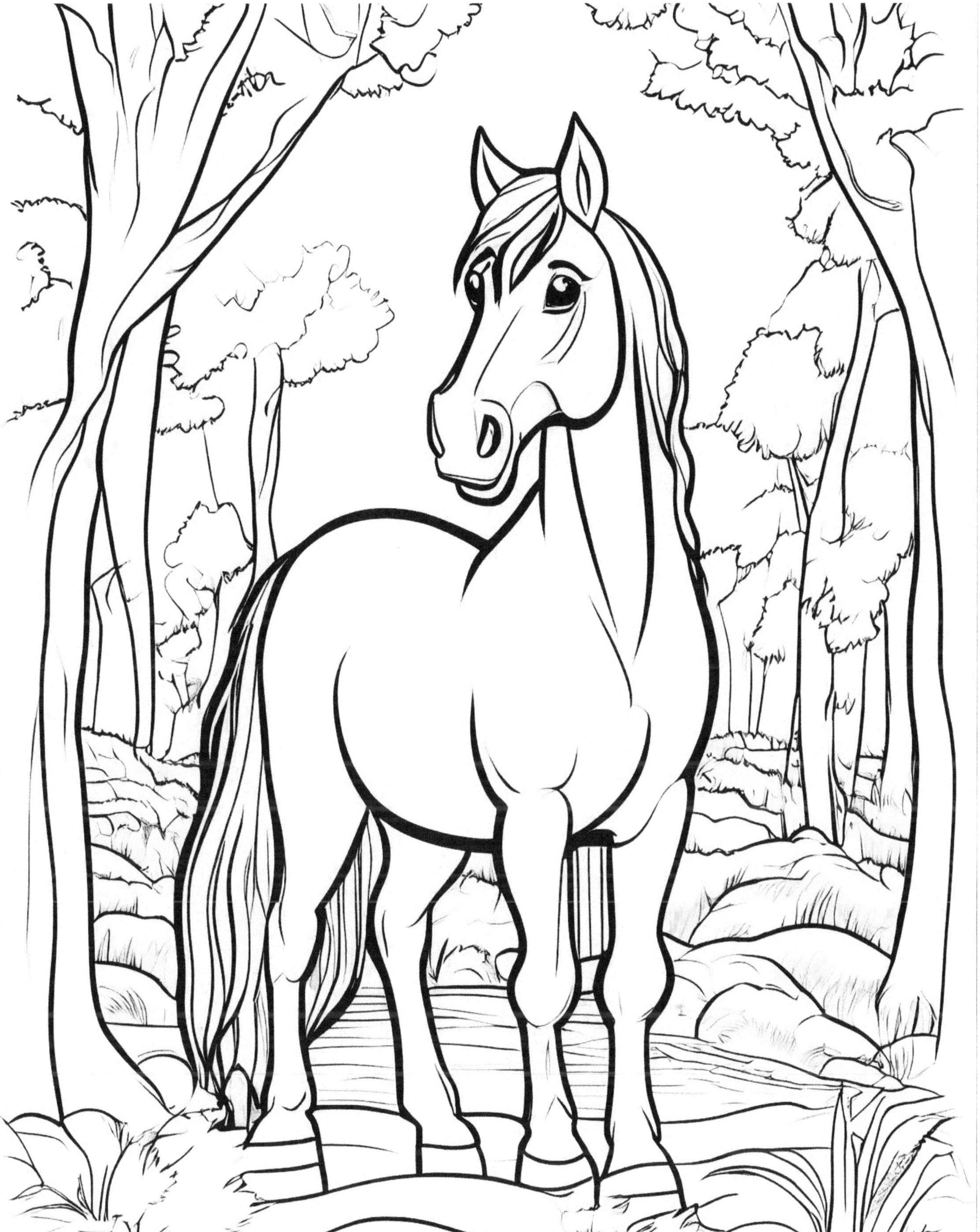

HORSE

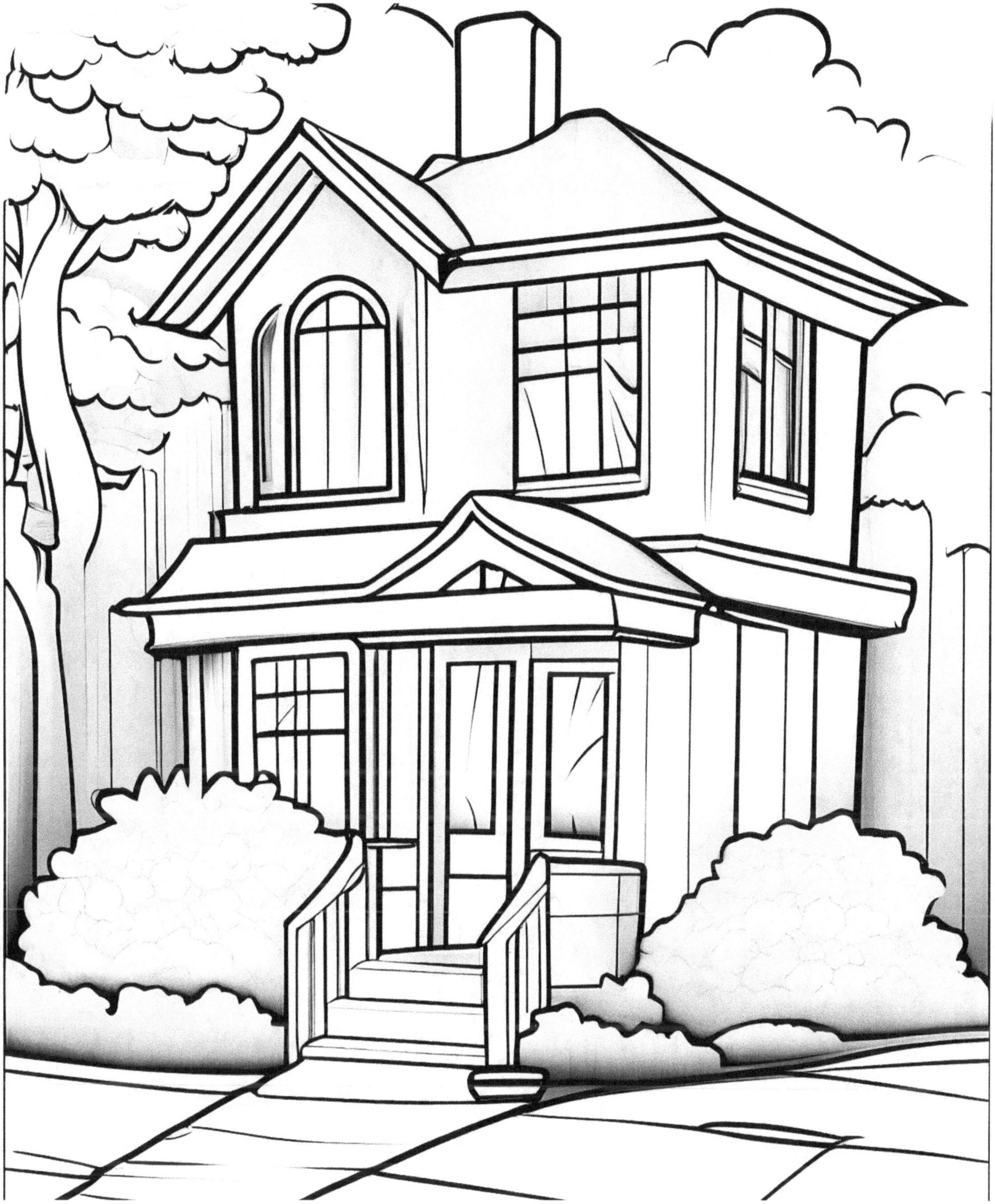

HOUSE

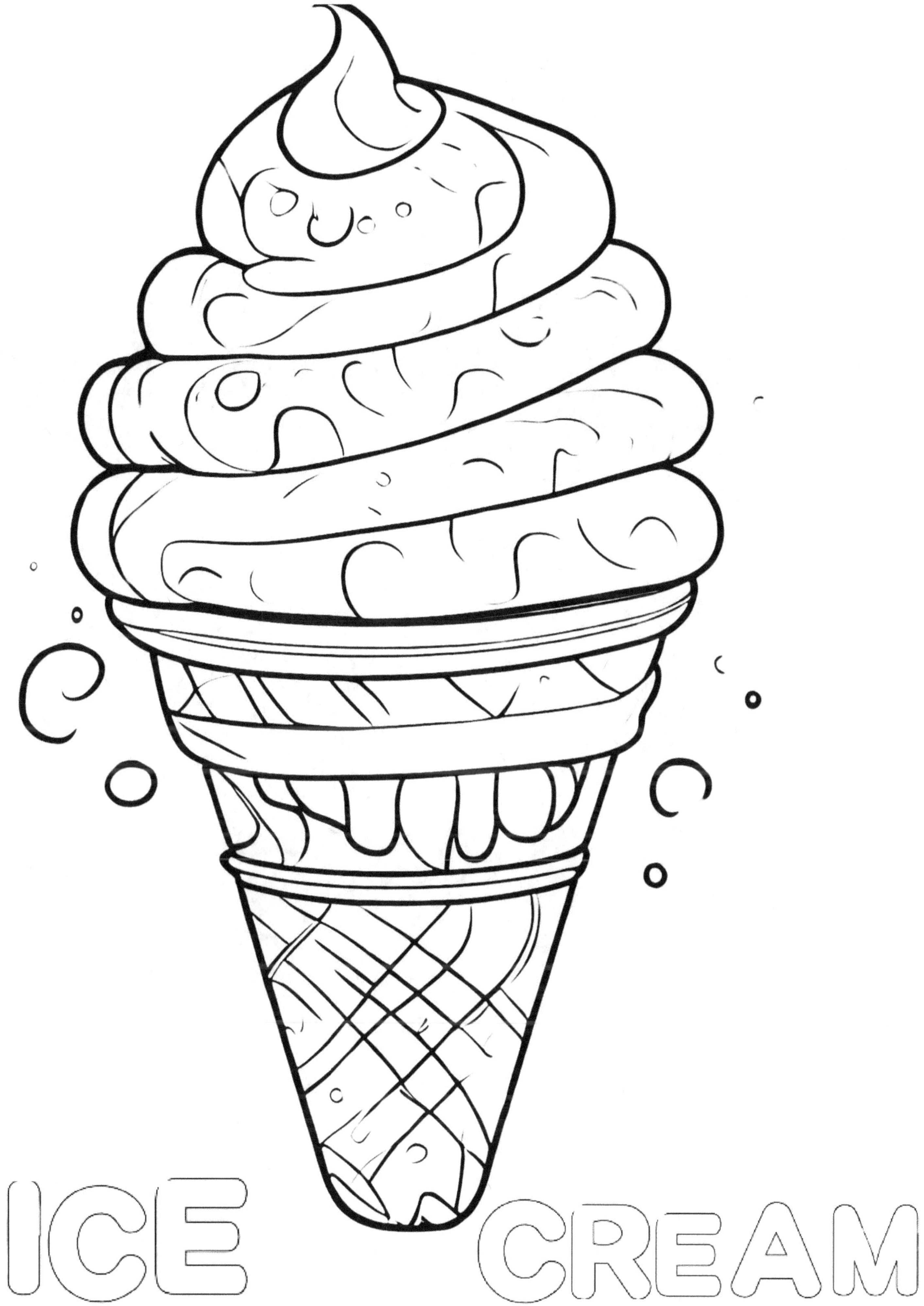
ICE CREAM

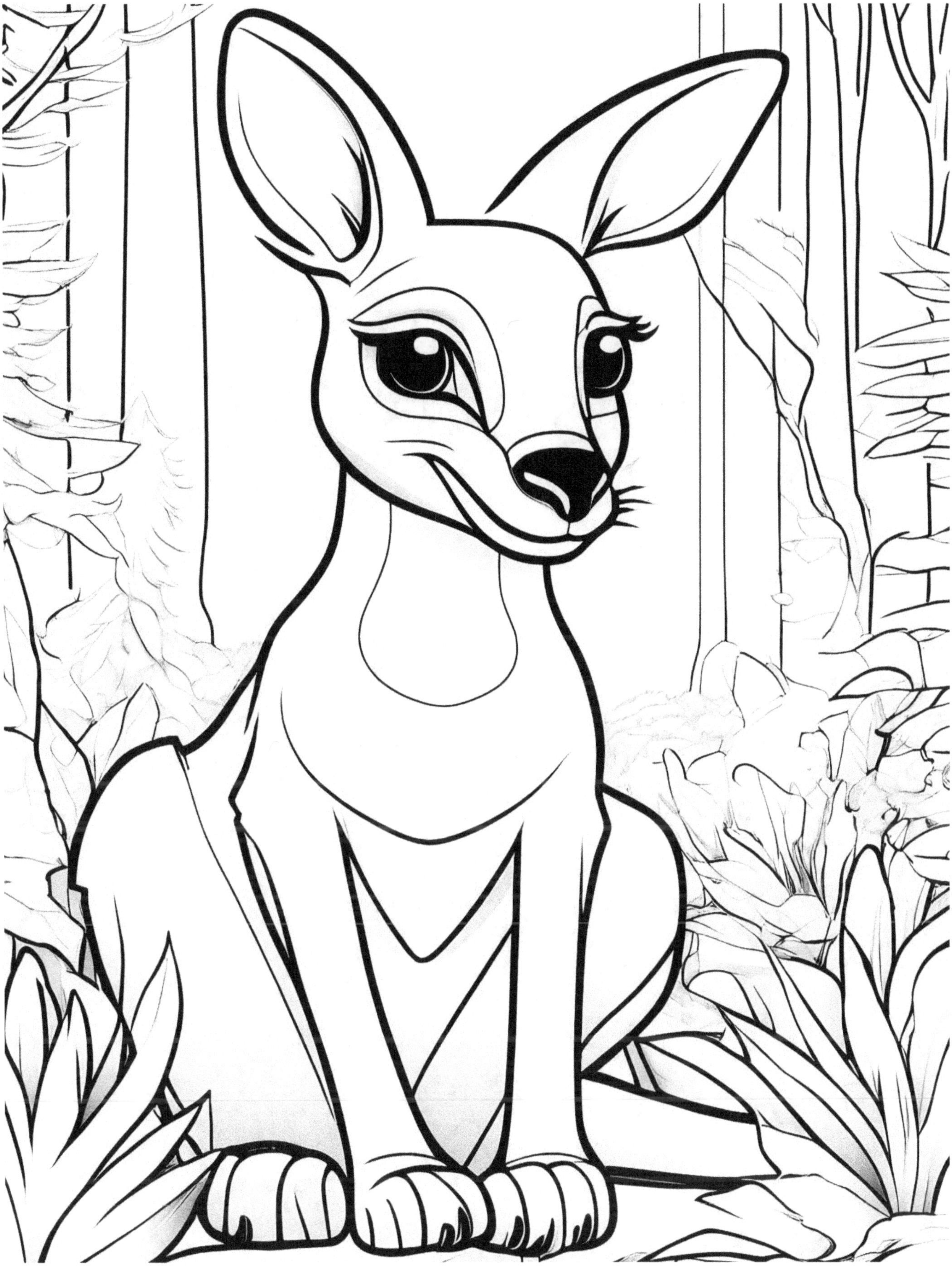

KANGAROO

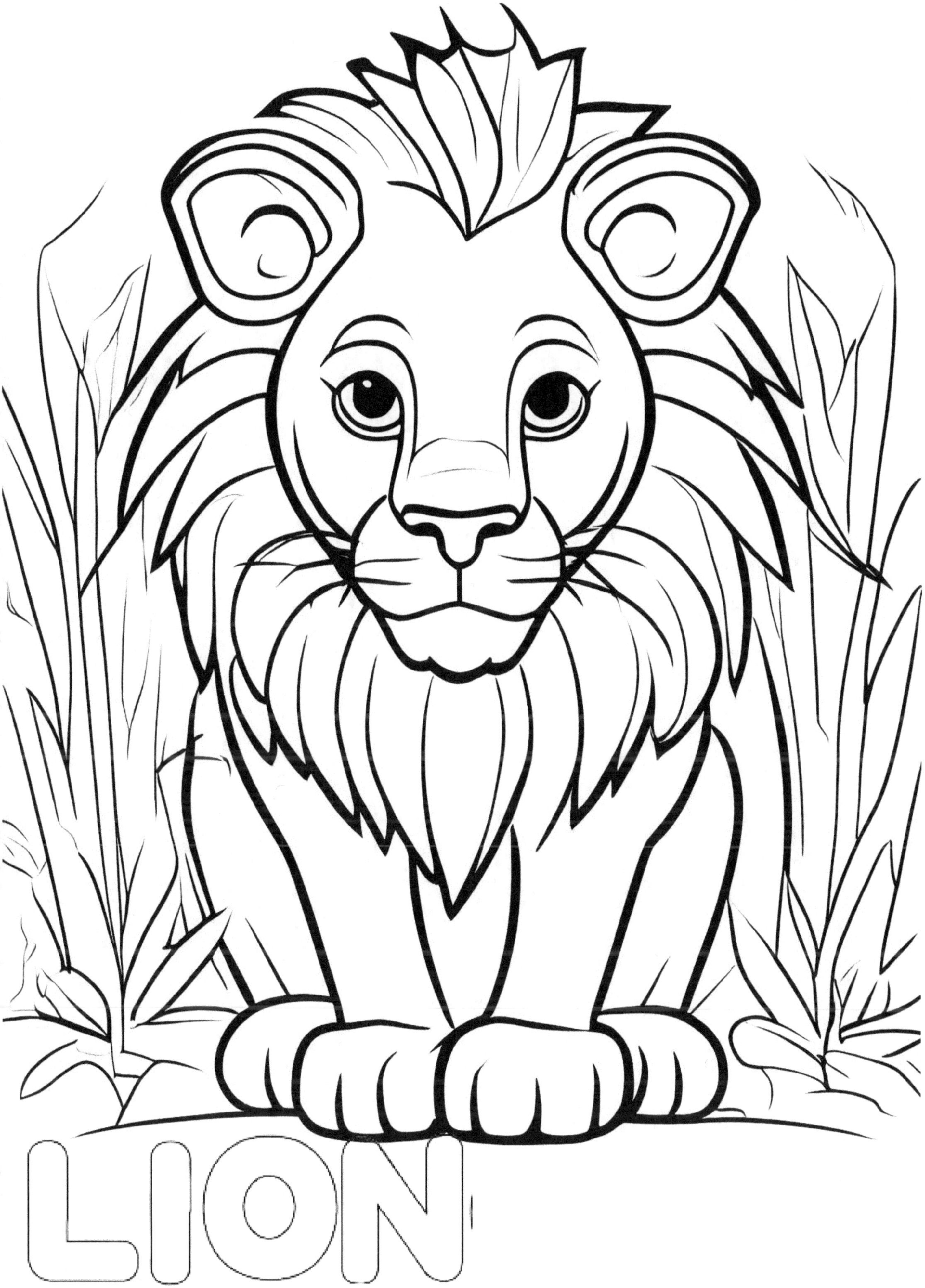

LION

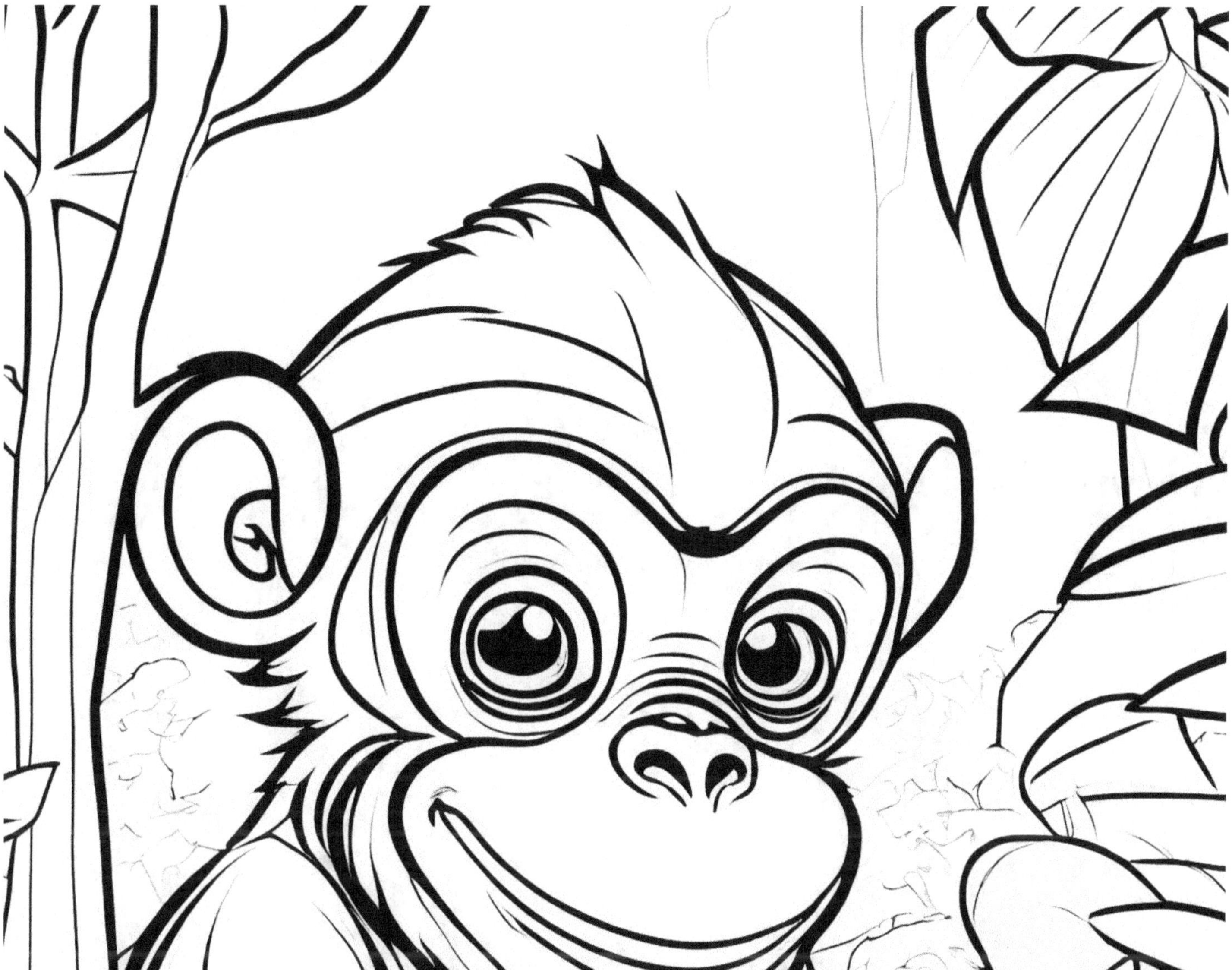

MONKEY

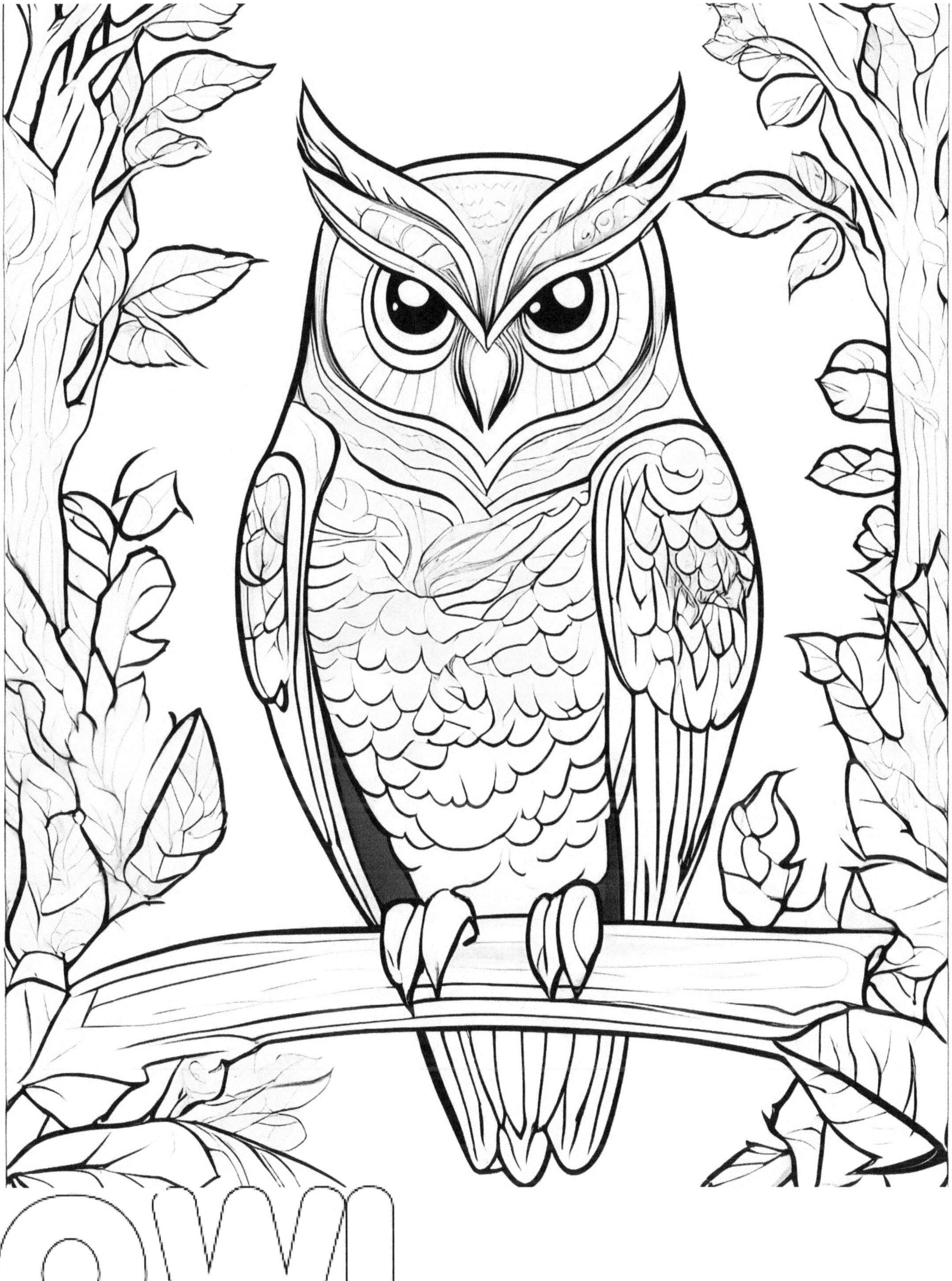

OWL

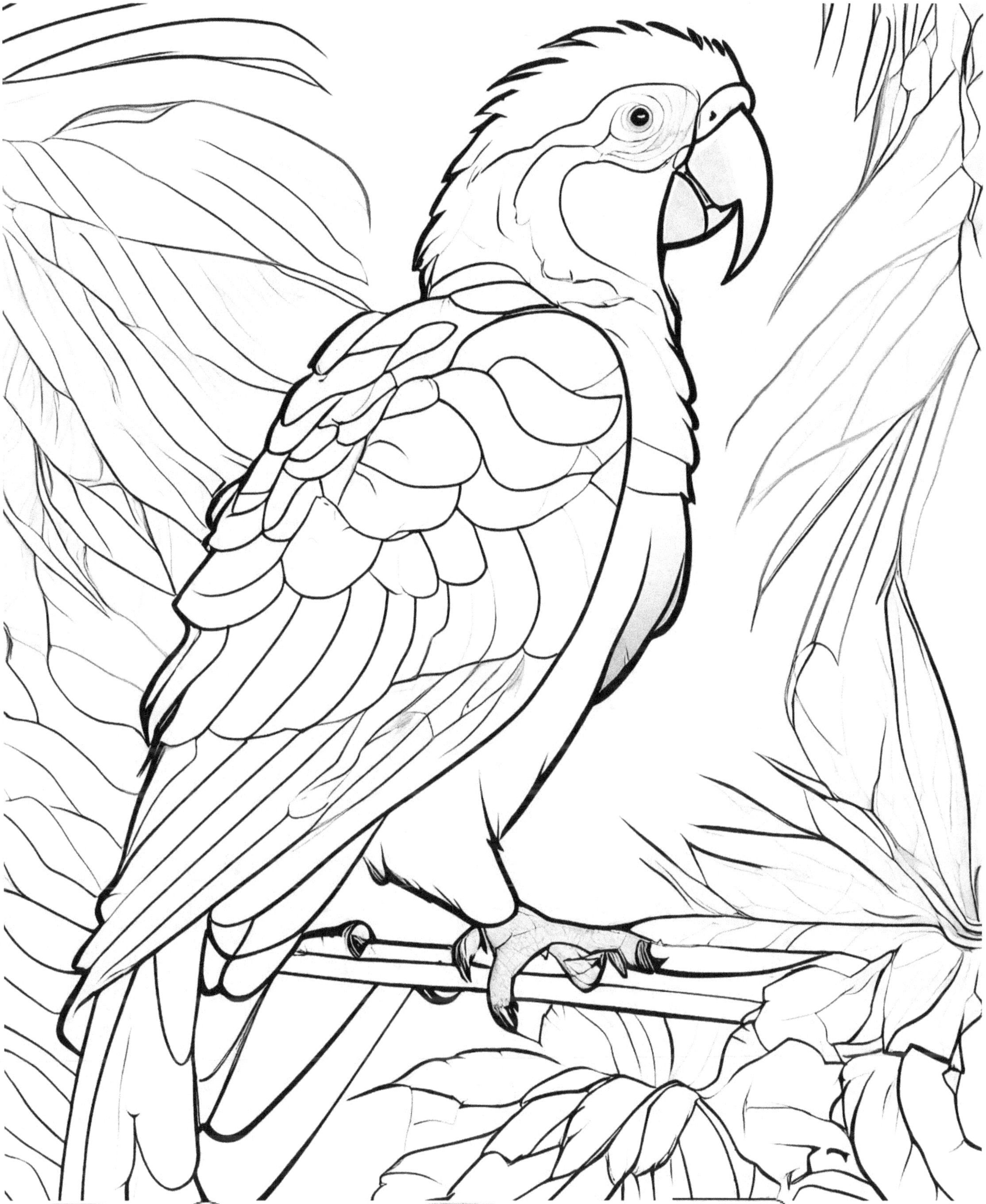

PARROT

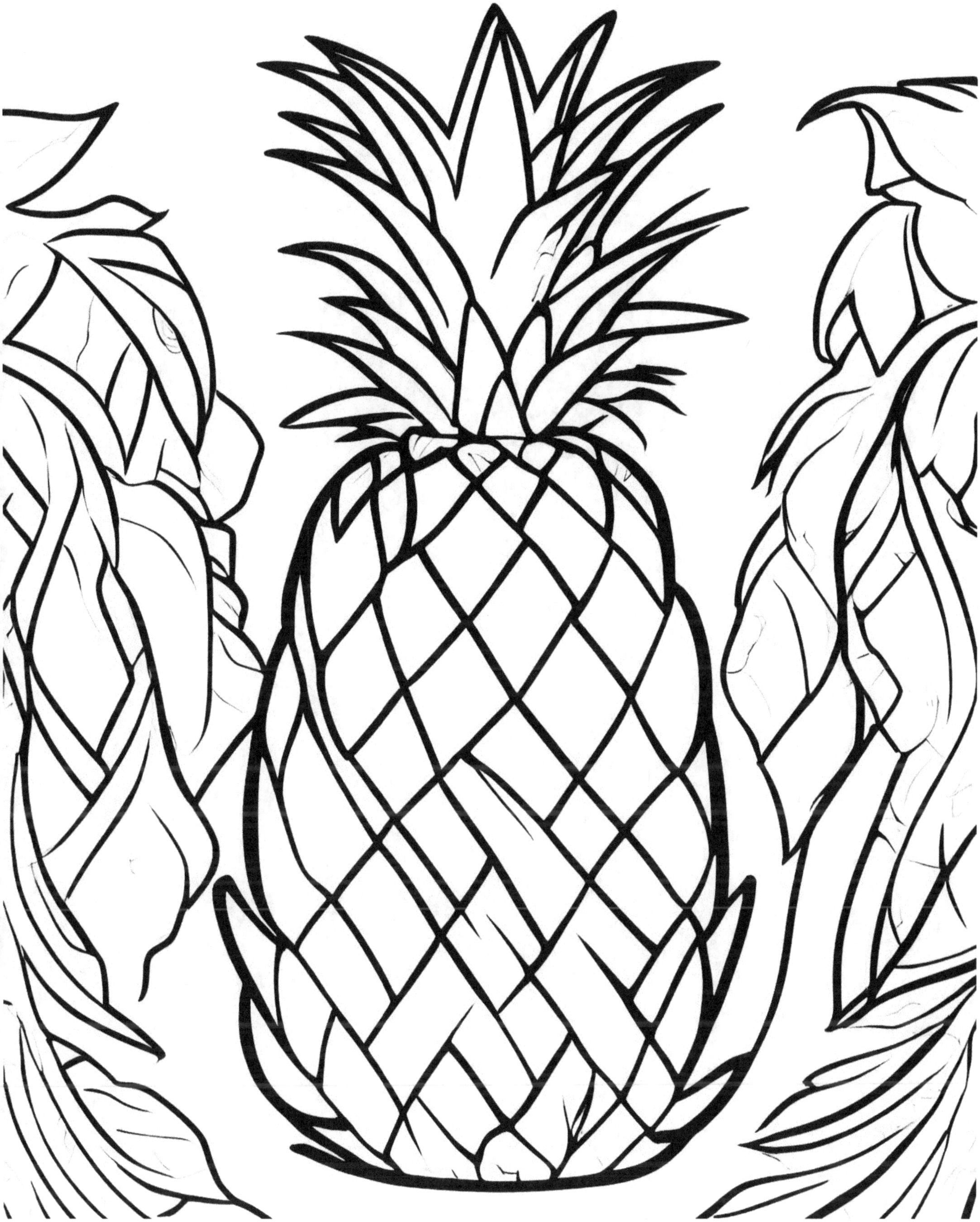

PINEAPLE

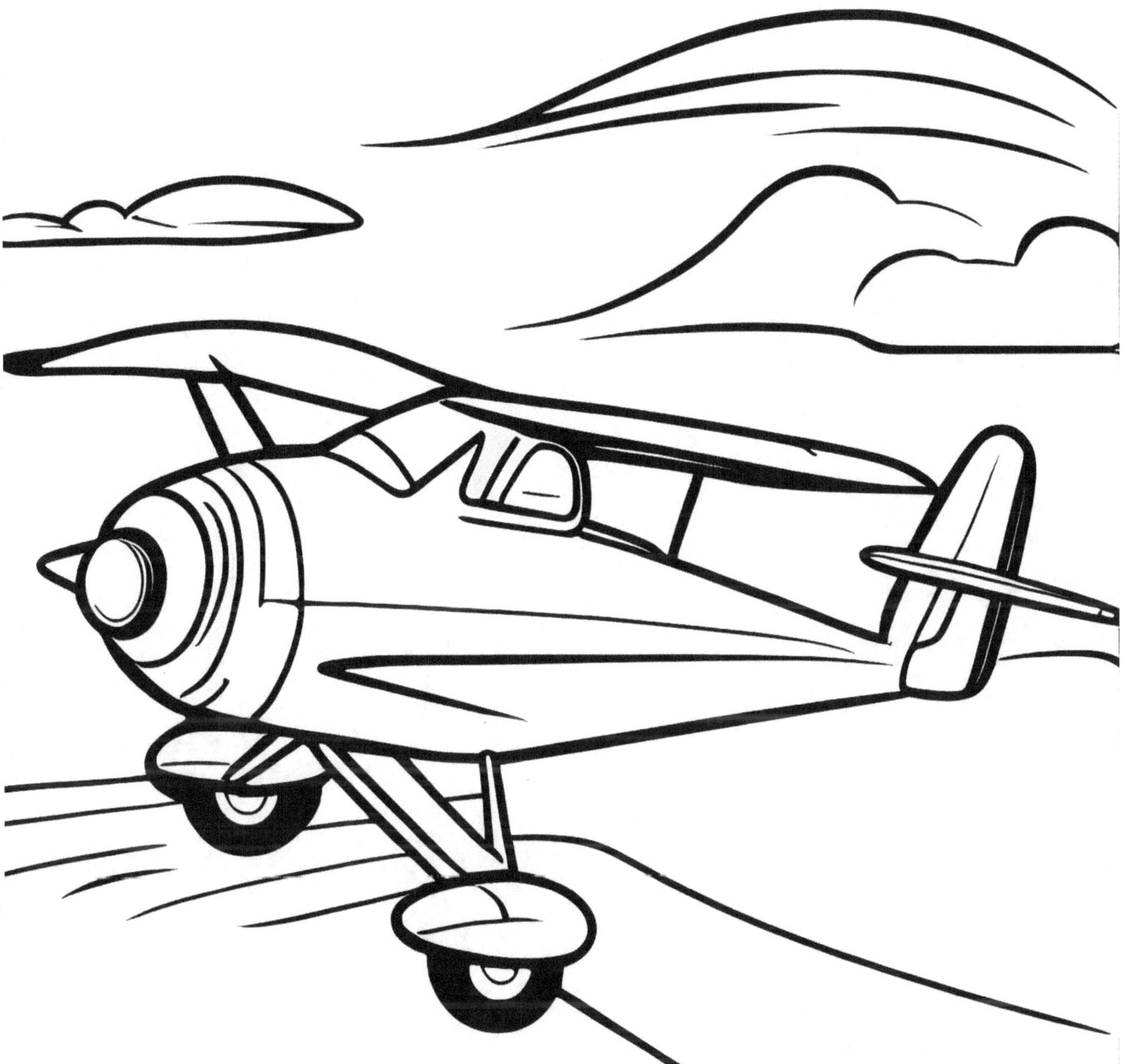

PLANE

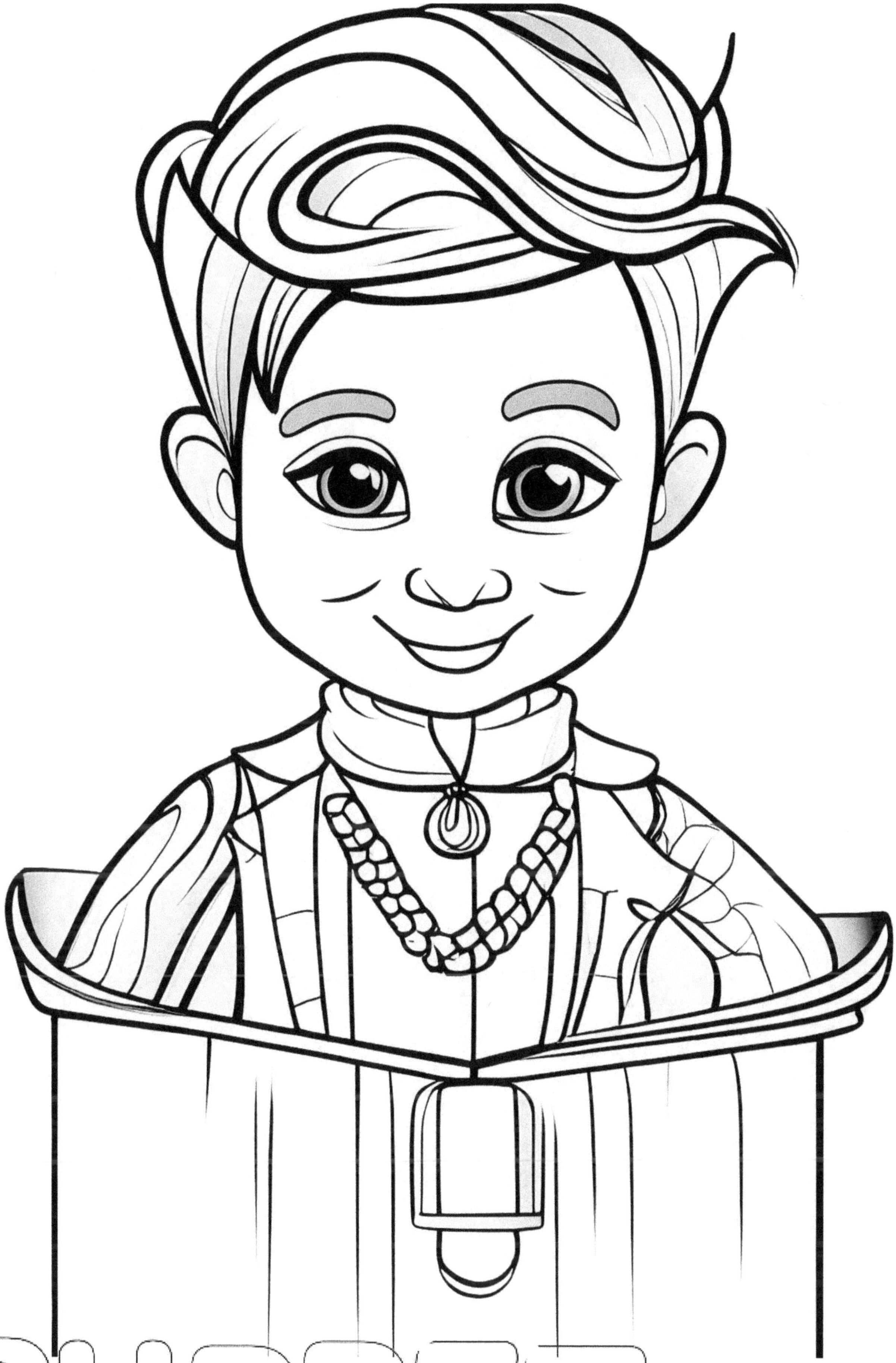

PUPPET

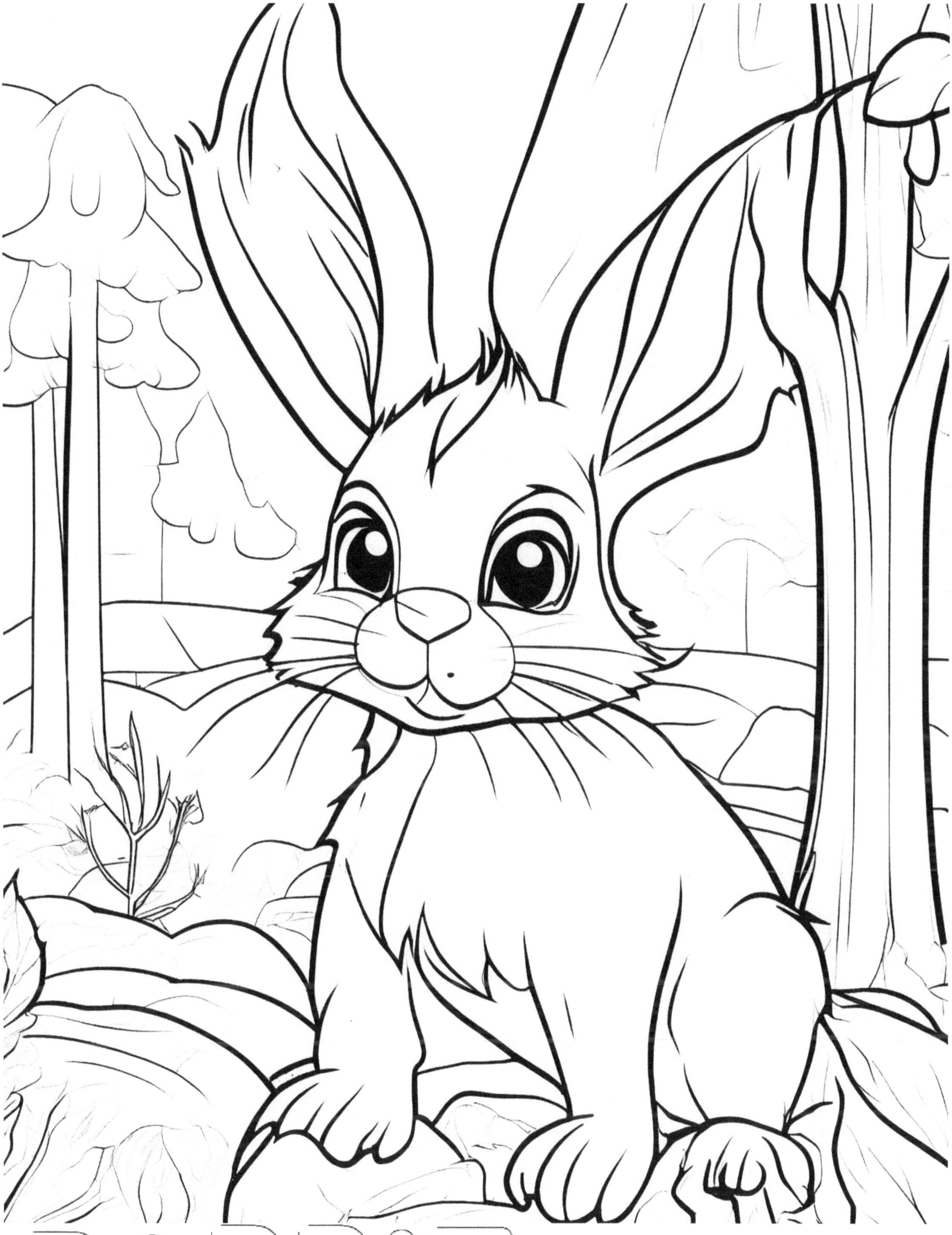

RABBIT

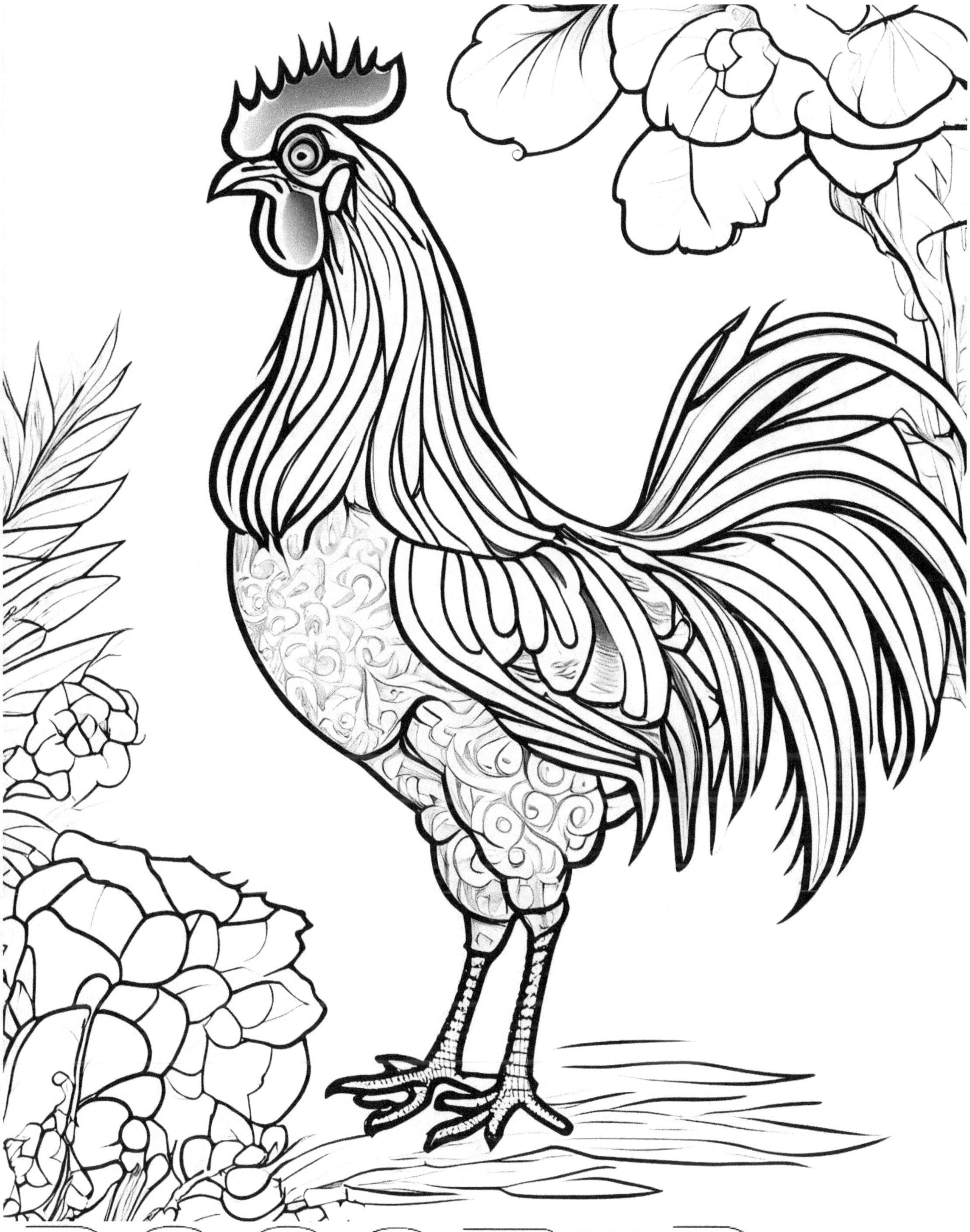

ROOSTER

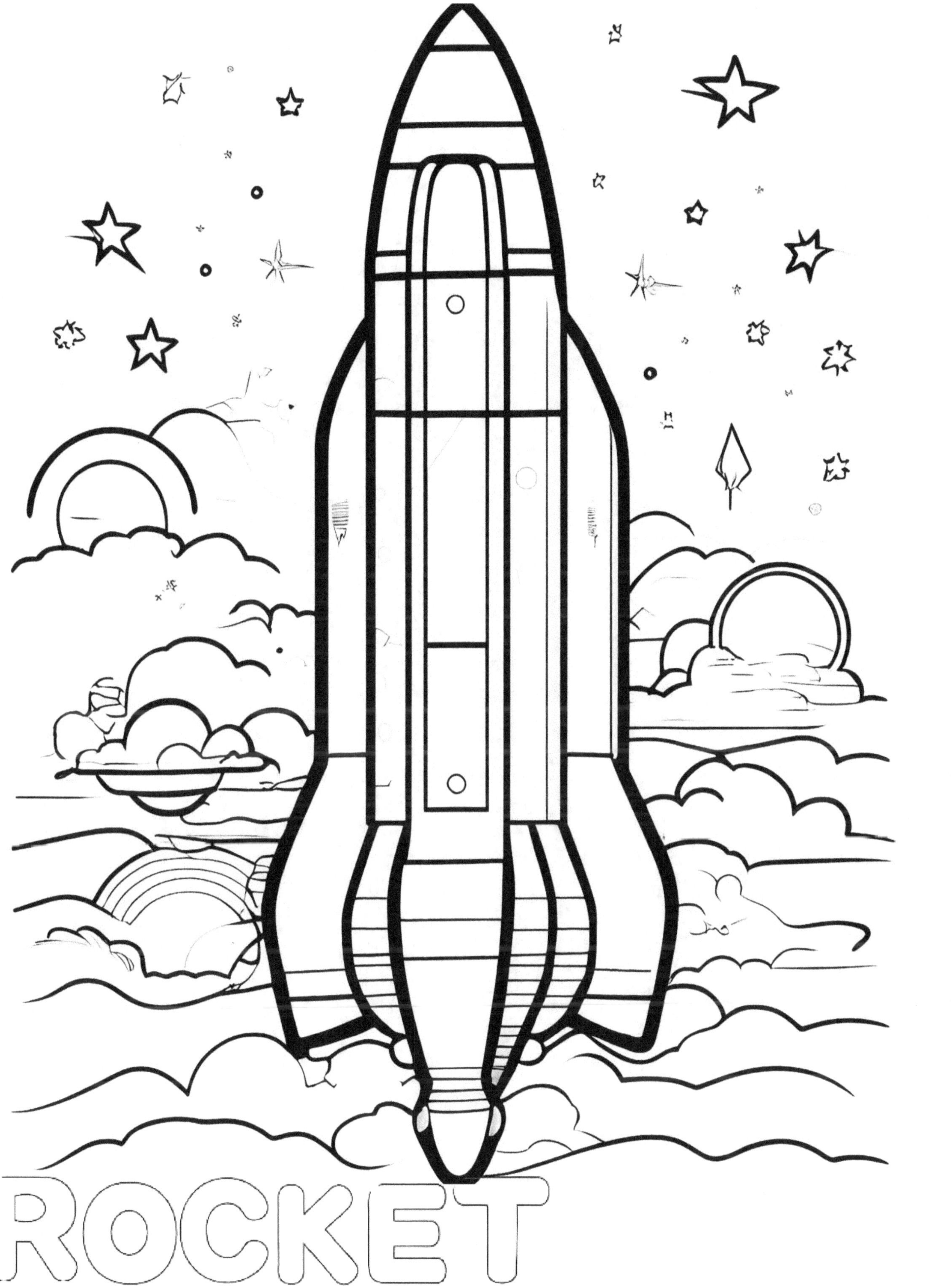

ROCKET

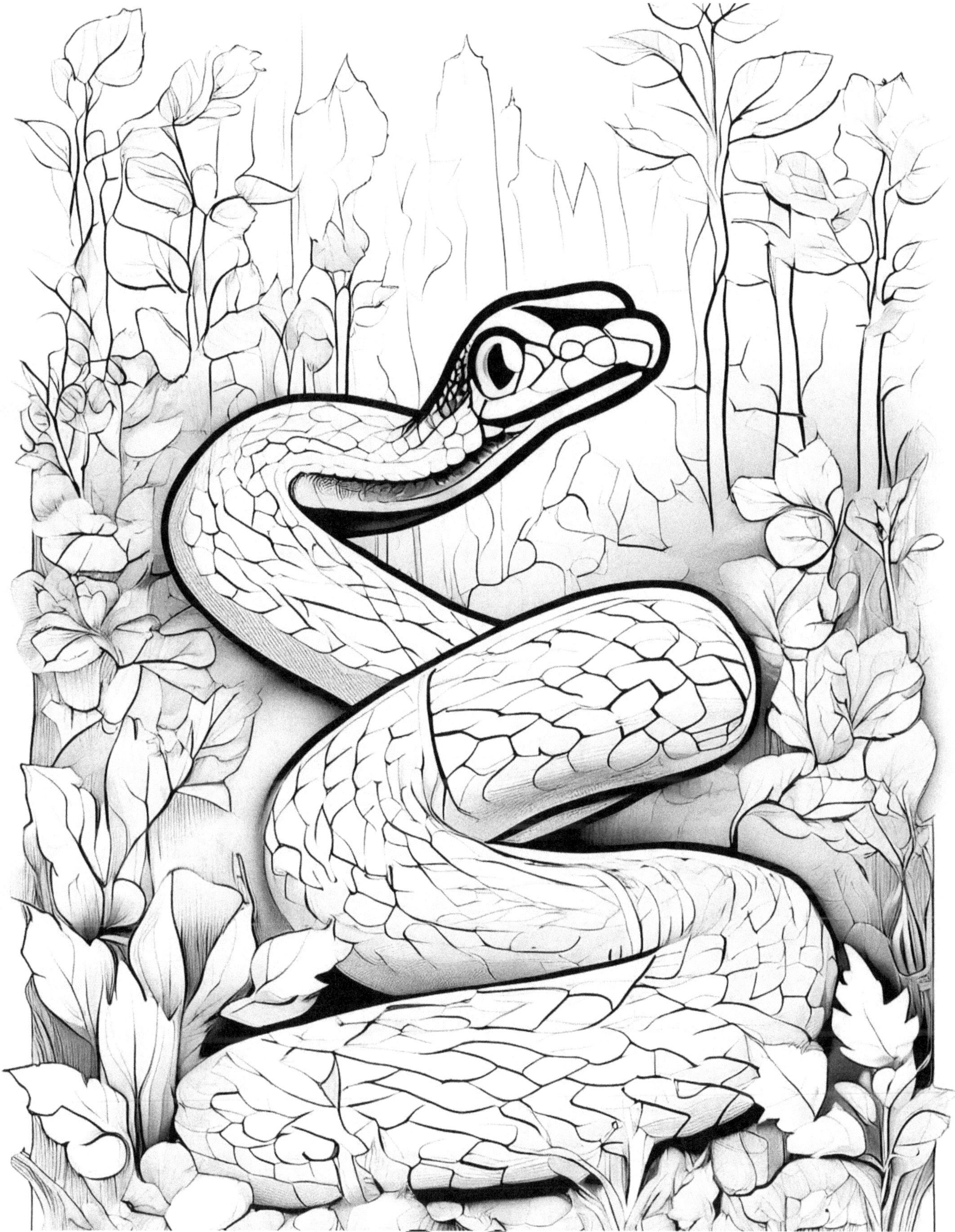

SNAKE

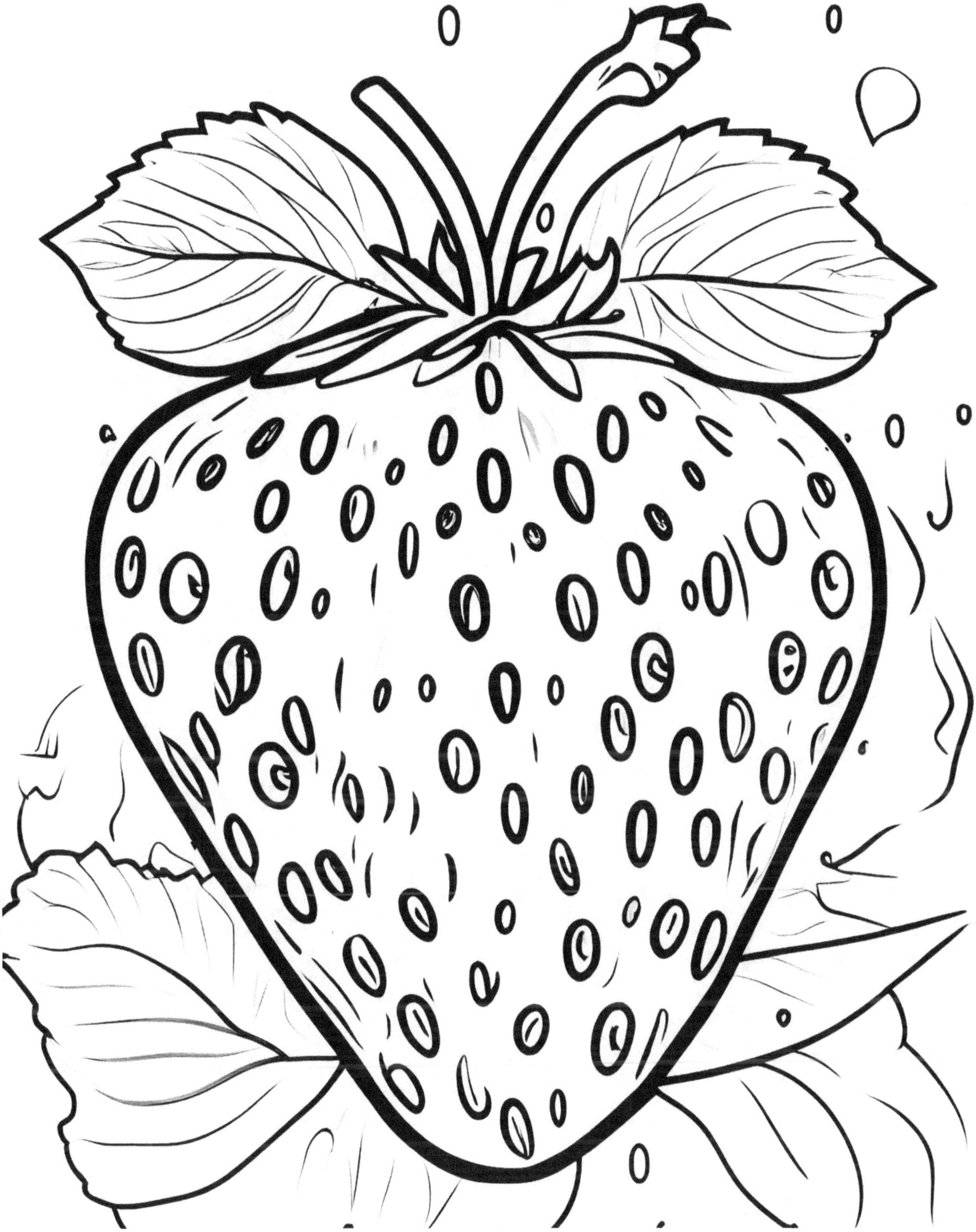

STRAWBERRY

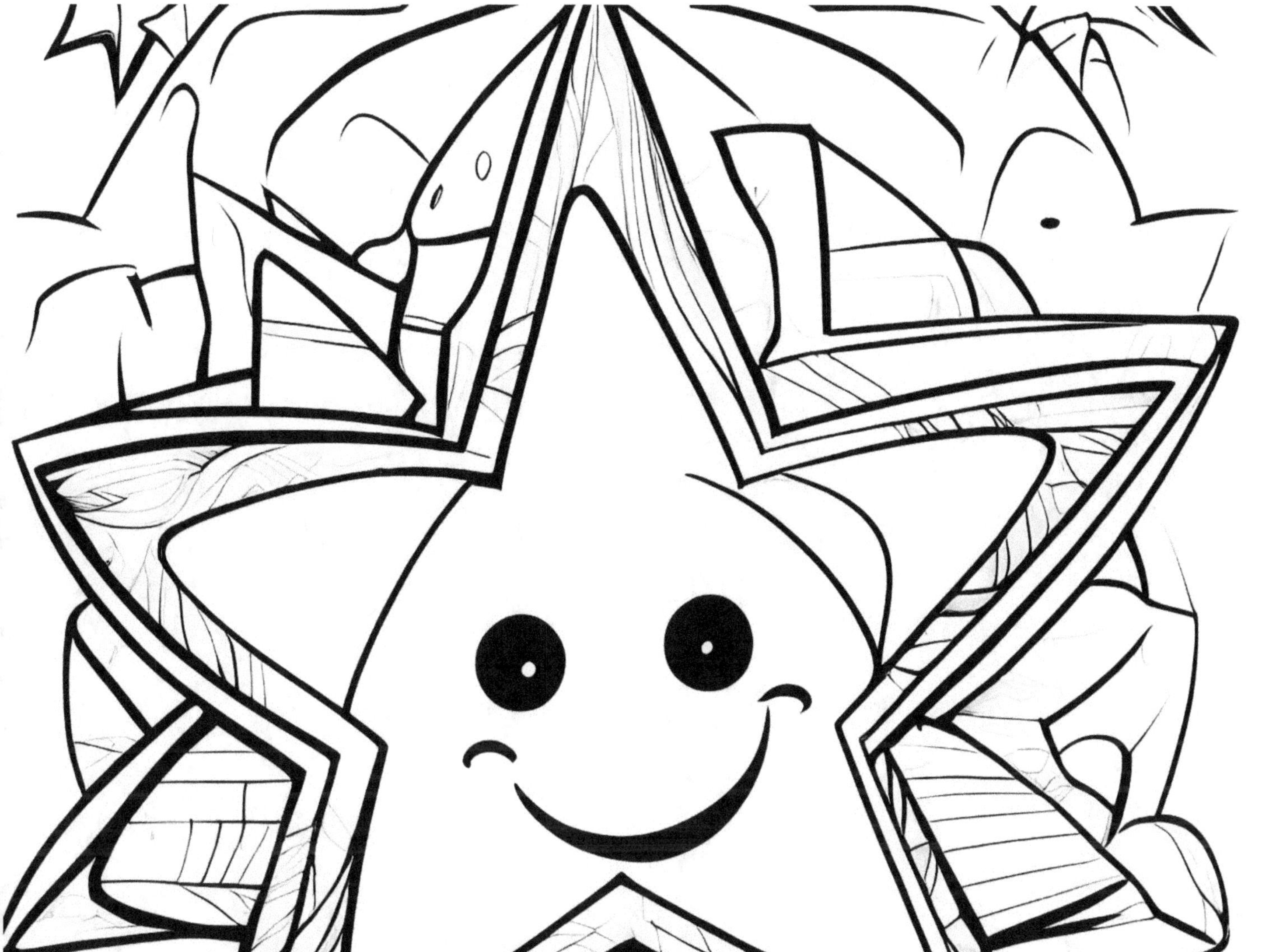

STAR

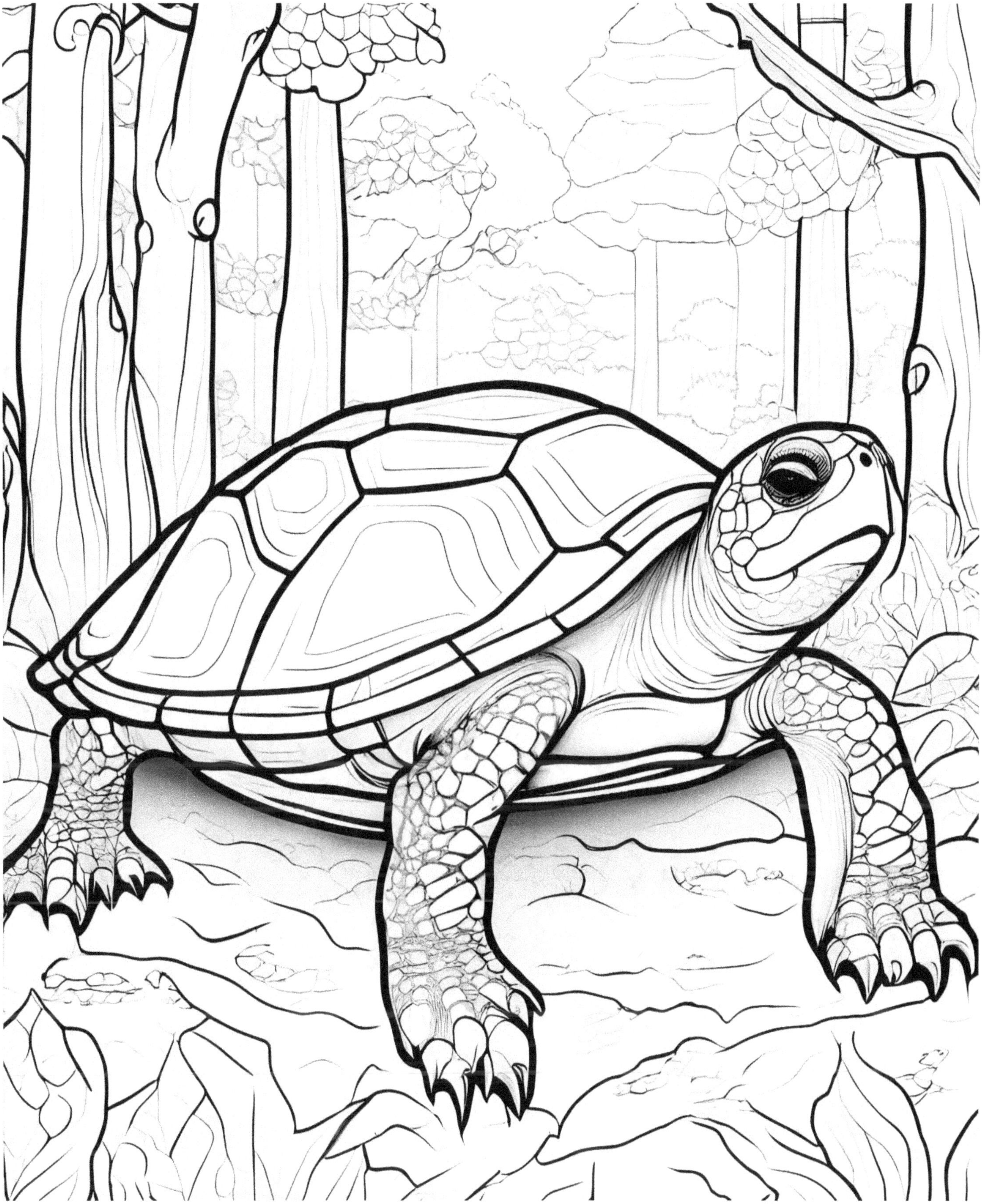

TURTLE

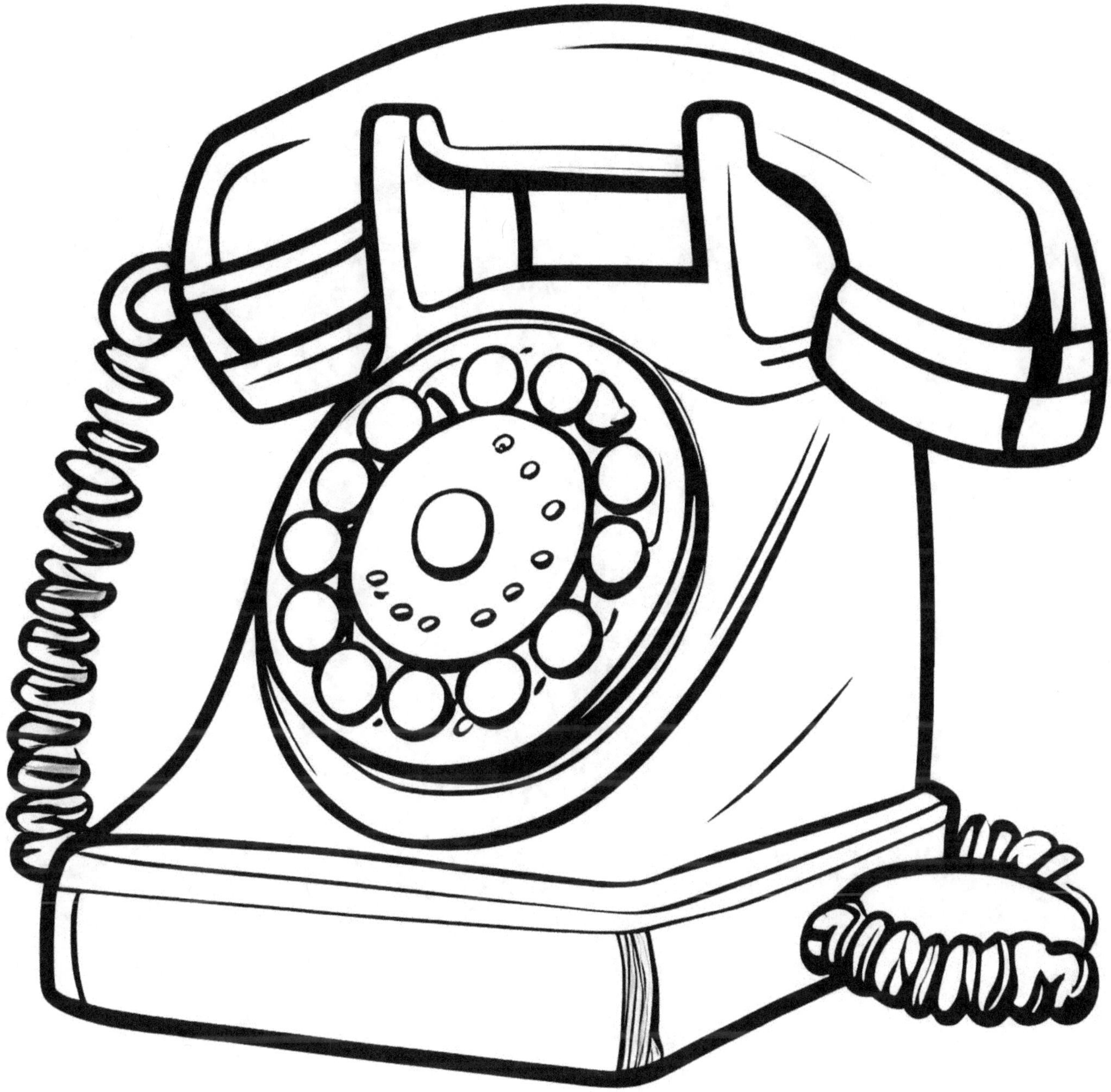

TELEPHONE

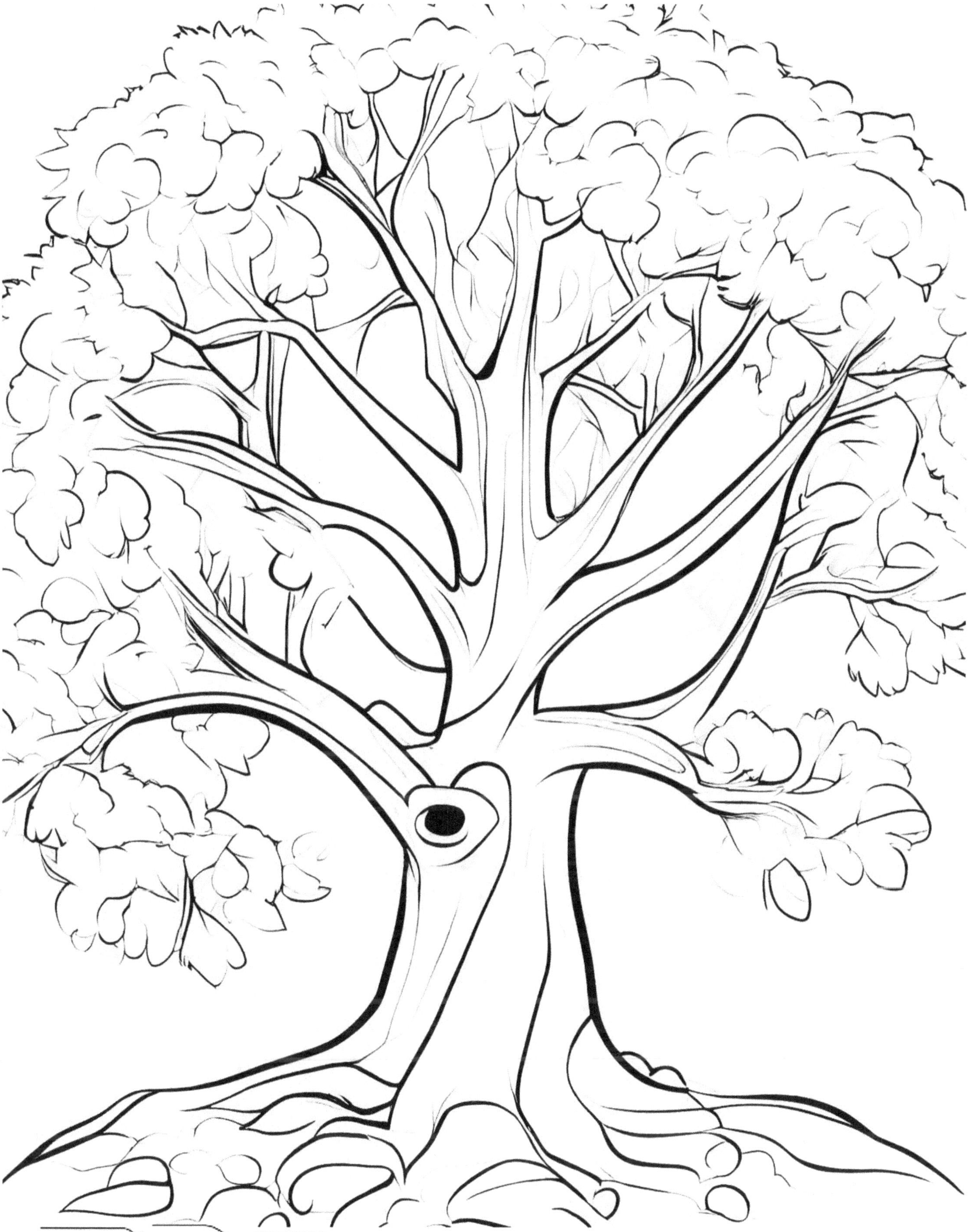

TREE

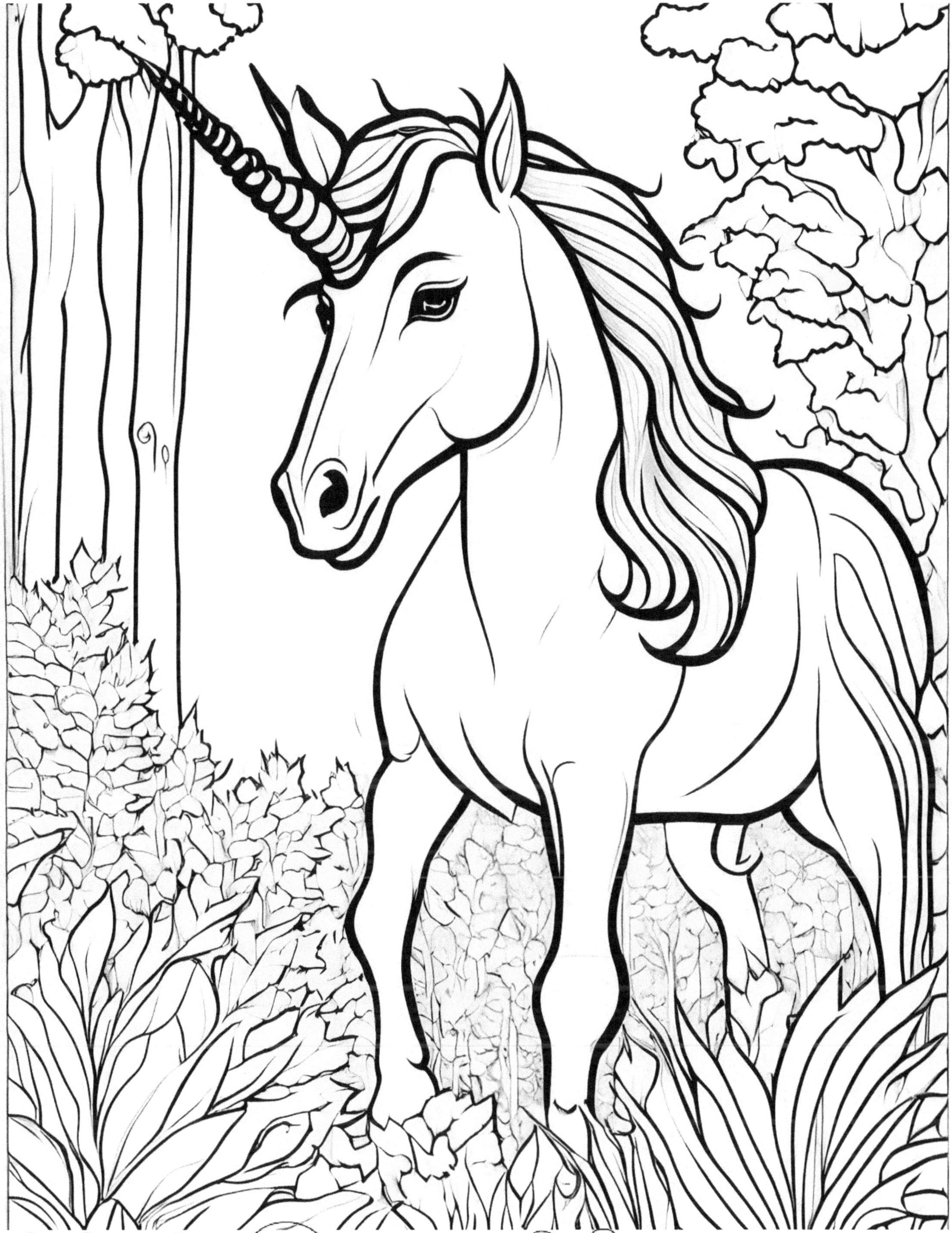

UNICORN

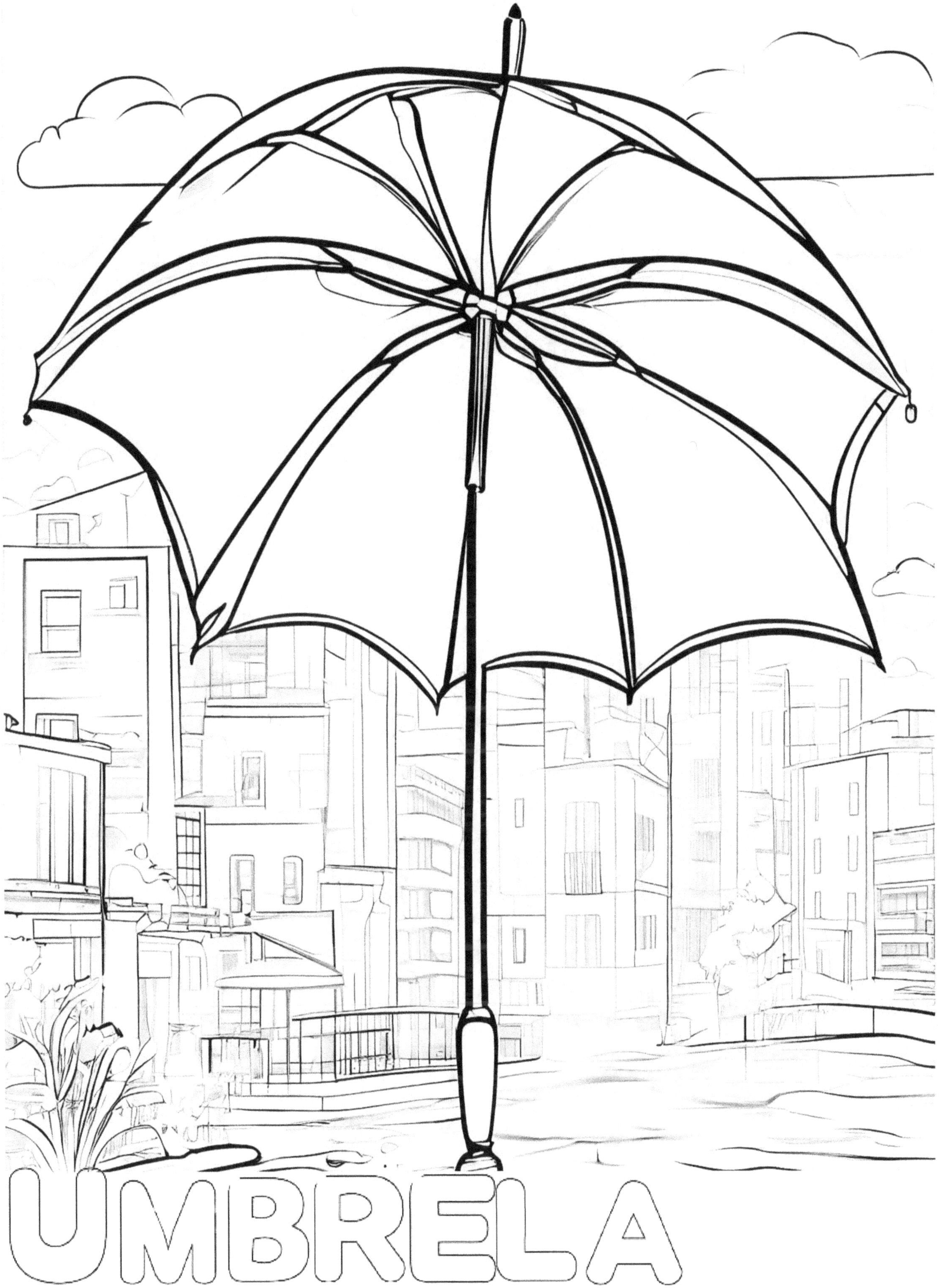

UMBRELA

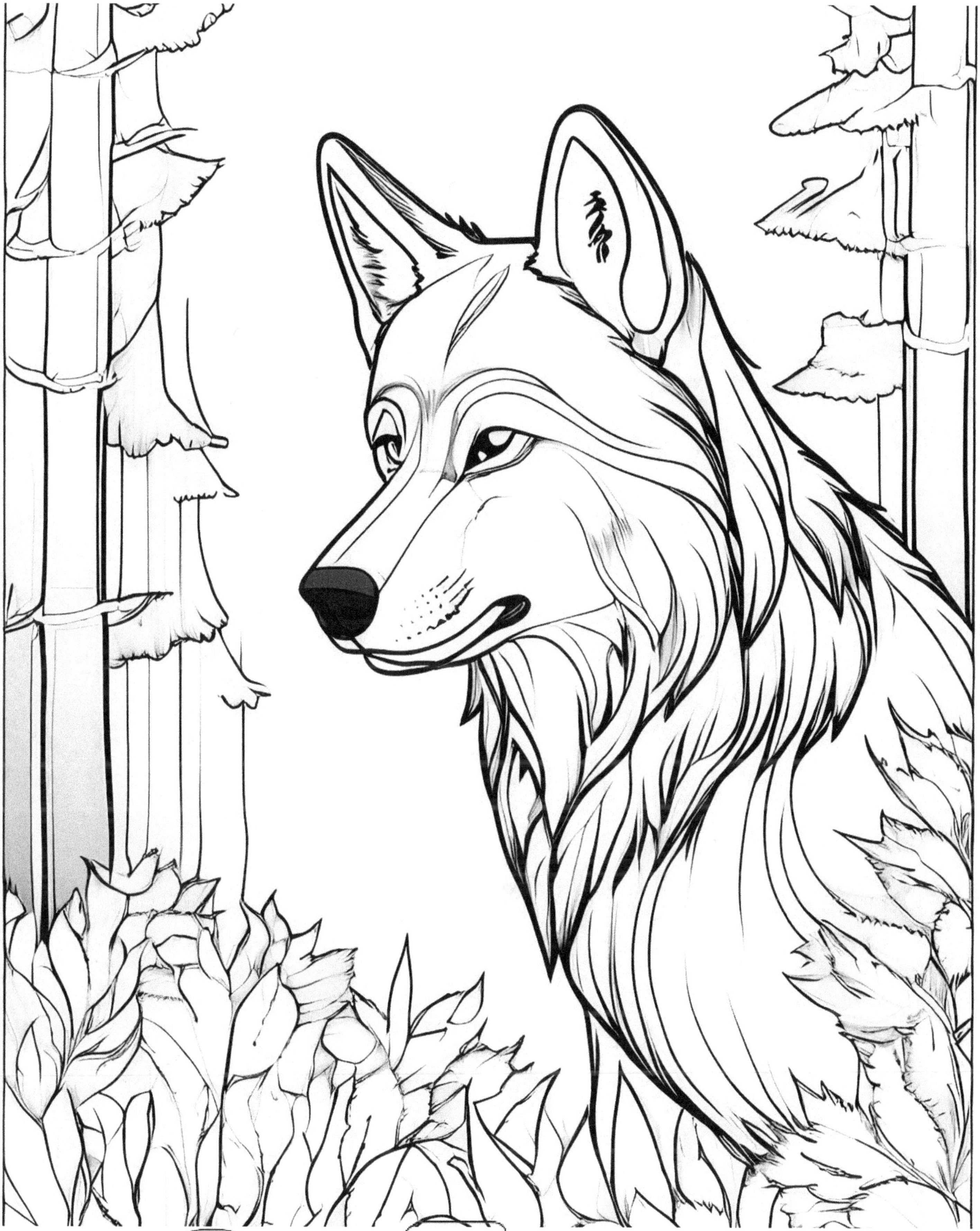

WOLF

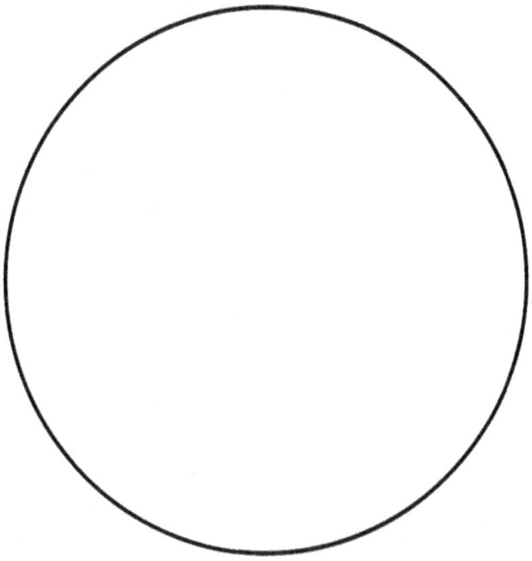

CIRCLE

SQUARE

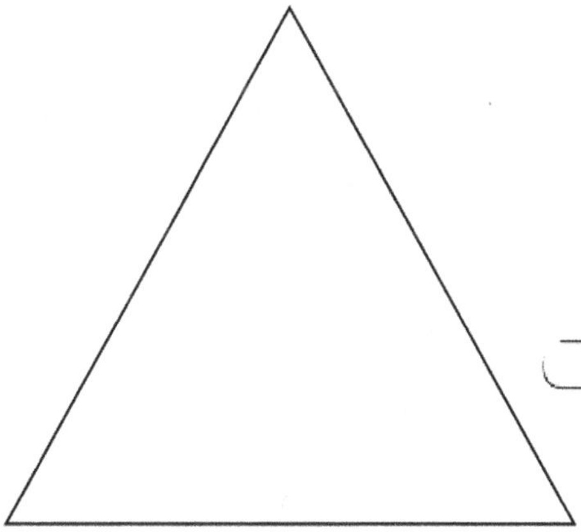

TRIANGLE

A B C

D E F

G H I

J K L

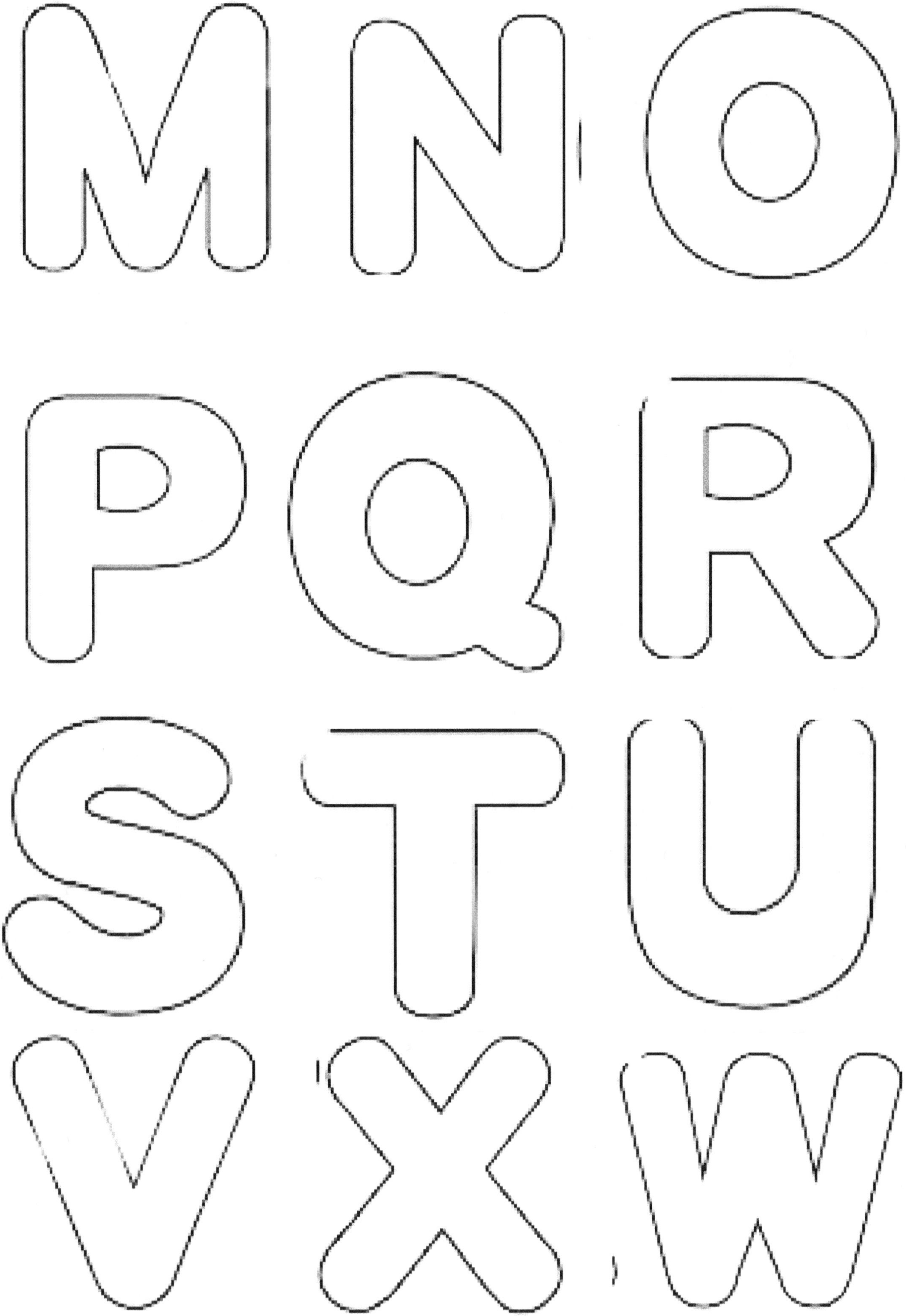
M N O
P Q R
S T U
V X W

Y Z

www.ingramcontent.com/pod-product-compliance
Lightning Source LLC
Chambersburg PA
CBHW082213220526
45470CB00010B/3157
* 9 7 9 8 3 2 5 6 7 1 1 3 5 *